Quarterly Essay

Quarterly Essay is published four times a year by Black Inc., an imprint of Schwartz Books Pty Ltd. Publisher: Morry Schwartz.

ISBN 9781760645793 ISSN 1444-884x

Subscriptions – 1 year print & digital (4 issues): $99.99 within Australia incl. GST. Outside Australia $134.99. 1 year digital only: $64.99.

Payment may be made by Mastercard or Visa, or by cheque made out to Schwartz Books. Payment includes postage and handling.

To subscribe, fill out and post the subscription card or form inside this issue, or subscribe online:

quarterlyessay.com
subscribe@quarterlyessay.com
Phone: 61 3 9486 0288

Correspondence should be addressed to:

The Editor, Quarterly Essay
22–24 Northumberland Street
Collingwood VIC 3066 Australia
Phone: 61 3 9486 0288 / Fax: 61 3 9011 6106
Email: quarterlyessay@blackincbooks.com

Editor: Chris Feik. Management: Elisabeth Young. Publicity: Anna Lensky. Design: Guy Mirabella. Associate Editor: Kirstie Innes-Will. Production Coordinator: Marilyn de Castro. Typesetting: Typography Studio.

Printed in Australia by McPherson's Printing Group.

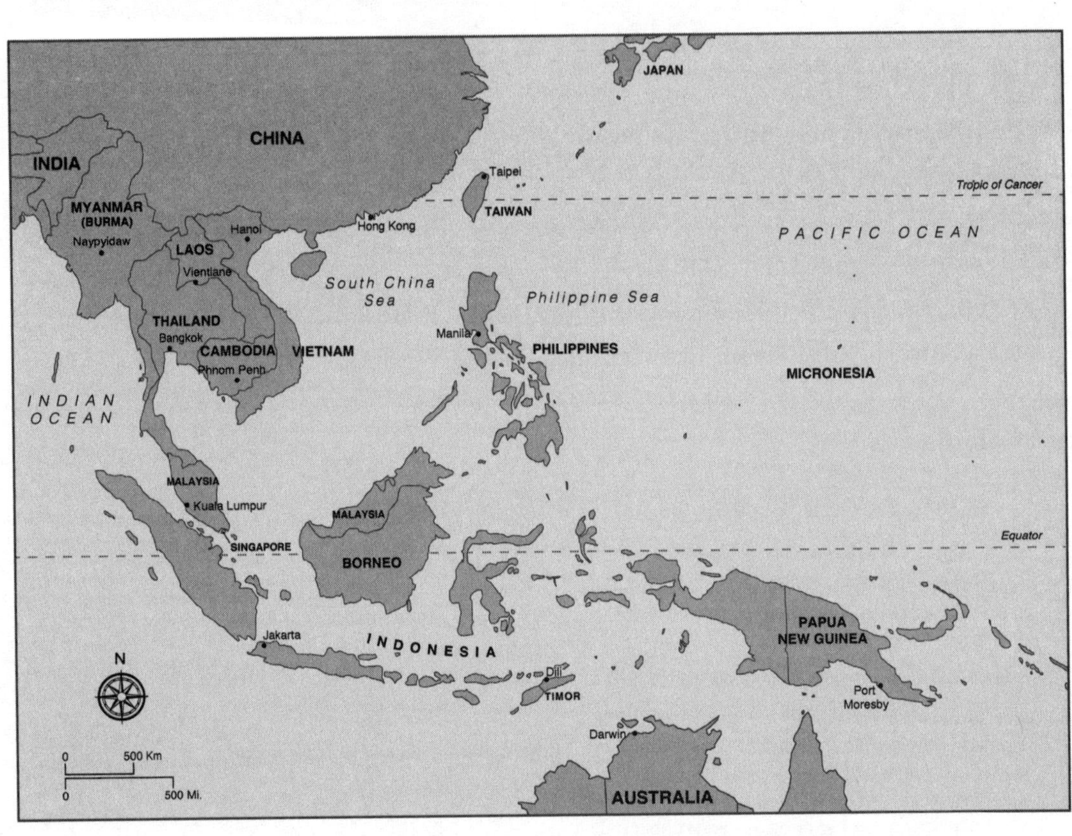
JAPAN
CHINA
INDIA
Taipei
Tropic of Cancer
MYANMAR
(BURMA)
Hanoi
TAIWAN
Hong Kong
PACIFIC OCEAN
Naypyidaw
LAOS
Vientiane
South China
Sea
Philippine Sea
THAILAND
Bangkok
Manila
CAMBODIA
VIETNAM
PHILIPPINES
Phnom Penh
MICRONESIA
INDIAN
OCEAN
MALAYSIA
Kuala Lumpur
MALAYSIA
Equator
SINGAPORE
BORNEO
PAPUA
NEW GUINEA
Jakarta
INDONESIA
N
Dili
TIMOR
Port
Moresby
Darwin
0
500 Km
0
500 Mi.
AUSTRALIA

BLIND SPOT

Southeast Asia and Australia's Future

Michael Wesley

On a hot, still, moonlit night in February, a Labor prime minister walks fretfully around the grounds of the Lodge in Canberra. Right on Australia's doorstep, an Asian great power has established a sphere of interest in Southeast Asia, proclaiming a new, anti-Western solidarity among former colonies. The prime minister knows that Australia has no capacity to defend itself: the bulk of our forces and equipment are committed to supporting our great ally's efforts far from the Australian continent. Until now, allied strategy has focused on defending a strategically located island, considered the keystone of our defence, but catastrophe has ensued: the island has been captured easily with the loss of hundreds of thousands of allied troops. The prime minister has been in increasingly acrimonious discussion with the leader of Australia's main ally – a vain, capricious and moody man, jealous of his power and prerogatives, convinced he is a master strategist. He insists Australia and its region are a secondary concern to the main theatre of competition and urges the prime minister to stay the course behind allied grand strategy. The Asian great power can either attack Australia directly or isolate it from the outside world by cutting off all shipping and air links.

The prime minister is John Curtin. The year is 1942. In the space of a month, imperial Japanese forces had easily seized Singapore, the keystone of British strategy in Asia, which, despite its repeated assurances otherwise,

Whitehall was unwilling and unable to defend. The Japanese had overrun the Dutch East Indies and Australian-administered New Guinea and reached into Solomon Islands. Darwin, Broome and other cities in northern Australia had been bombed. The bulk of Australia's forces and equipment were fighting in North Africa, leaving it essentially undefended. Despite the desperation of Australia's position, British and American leaders had met in Washington and agreed that the war against the Nazis had priority, and no measure should be taken to defend Australia that would detract from the allied effort in Europe. In an increasingly bad-tempered exchange with the British prime minister, Winston Churchill, Curtin insisted Australian troops be withdrawn from North Africa to defend their own country. Even then, Churchill argued that Australian troops should be committed to Burma, to defend Britain's Indian colonies from Japan. Curtin prevailed, and the Australian troops returned to defend Australia.

History doesn't repeat itself, but it often rhymes, Mark Twain is reputed to have said. In the eighty-four years since a sleepless Curtin trudged around the gardens of the Lodge, Australia seems to have learnt little from the most profound strategic shock in its history. The rhymes of history are becoming more persistent and more pointed. Another Asian great power, vastly more capable than imperial Japan, is intent on developing a sphere of interest to Australia's immediate north, built around an anti-Western, "Asia for the Asians" appeal. Meanwhile, Australia's military capabilities have become as completely embedded in allied strategic planning as they were in 1942 – and focused on supporting American commitments a long way from Australia's shores. The biggest bet in Australian military history – a $368-billion wager on acquiring nuclear-powered submarines – locks Canberra into allied defence of another keystone island, Taiwan, while cannibalising all other defence capabilities. Again, we have become distracted from the strategic significance of the islands to our immediate north. Australia's standing and influence in Southeast Asia, the region of primary significance to Australia's future, is eroding quickly, as Canberra positions itself in the vanguard of efforts to contain China. Meanwhile, Australia cleaves ever more desperately to the US alliance, at a time when profound domestic shifts in the United States are recasting America's role in the world. Anthony Albanese probably isn't retracing Curtin's night-time pacing around the garden of the Lodge. But he should be.

*

Australia nestles at the southern end of the longest archipelago on the planet. This chain of more than 50,000 islands stretches for over 7000 kilometres along the eastern coastline of the world's largest, most populous and richest continent: Asia. From the Aleutian Islands in the north, the great archipelago extends south through Japan, the Ryukus, Taiwan, Micronesia, the Philippines, Indonesia and New Guinea, to Australia. It then curves eastwards into the middle of the Pacific, through Melanesia and Polynesia.

Australia's archipelagic location is our most profound and enduring strategic reality. The vast bulk of the mineral, energy and agricultural exports that make us wealthy pass between the islands to our immediate north. The fuel supplies that are the lifeblood of Australian society make their way south towards our ports through the same waterways. A traveller by air to Asia, Europe or the Middle East has to fly through the airspace above those islands. And as we saw in 1942, the most serious threats to Australia's security will manifest in or through the chain of islands between the Asian continent and our own.

This is an essay about how we overlook this most basic, most fundamental fact, which holds the key to Australia's future safety and prosperity. The islands, coasts and waterways to our north have been nominated as the region of primary importance in every strategic planning document since the 1950s. Having acknowledged this reality, however, Australian governments then regularly proceed to forget it. In the past decade, the problem has become worse, as the frameworks of threat and reassurance Australia have adopted are increasingly at odds with those of its most important neighbours. This has occurred when Southeast Asia is becoming more contested, and when the assets Australia has hitherto relied on to give it authority and influence are rapidly depreciating.

Australia's governments and society suffer from a form of strategic long-sightedness – hyperopia, the opposite of myopia. We tend to overlook

Southeast Asia and focus on relationships and situations further from our shores. Culturally, we are ever more embedded in Europe and North America; economically, our major trade partners are in Northeast Asia and, increasingly, India; our political and diplomatic attention follows those whom we comfortingly designate as "like-minded." Strategically, our commitments increasingly follow the whims and evolving postures of our American ally – which tends to see Southeast Asia as a backwater.

Australia's current thinking in effect ignores the foundational geopolitical impulse of colonial Australia. From the mid-nineteenth century, the Australian colonies began to voice fears about hostile interests lodging in the islands to Australia's north and northeast, serving as bases from which the colonies could be attacked. These fears, and a frustration that Britain wasn't taking them seriously, were a major impetus towards Federation and, nine years later, the creation of an Australian navy.

From their earliest strategic imaginings, the colonists saw the great island chain as both an avenue of attack and a rampart of defence. The islands to the immediate north and northeast – in today's terminology, maritime Southeast Asia and Melanesia – became a particular focus of attention. Before World War I, a report to government recommended that imperial forces should create a "flexible tripwire" in the islands between Australia and the Asian continent, to attack and defend against hostile forces. During World War II, Australian fears about those islands were realised, as imperial Japanese forces rapidly took Singapore, the Philippines, Micronesia, Indonesia, New Guinea and Solomon Islands, to be poised to strike the Australian continent.

The end of the war delivered Australia from the Japanese menace, but it also saw the old colonial order recede rapidly from the archipelago. No longer could certainty be determined by imperial agreement in the chancelleries of Europe. In 1954, Australia's foreign policy planners, grappling with the prospects of independent Asian and Pacific neighbours and the hardening of Cold War rivalries, defined as the top priority for Australian foreign policy, "To exert dominant political influence in the [Southeast Asian and Melanesian] area with a view to maintaining Australian security behind a peripheral screen of islands." It is a formula that has endured in defence planning, though changing in language and nuance, through the rapid evolution of the world beyond Australia's shores, and of Australian society itself. Fast forward seventy years, and the 2024 National Defence Strategy gives priority to "safeguarding Australia's interests in our primary areas of military interest, the immediate region encompassing the Northeast Indian Ocean through maritime Southeast Asia into the Pacific."

*

That original instinct – to view Australia as part of an extended archipelago that holds the keys to our security and defence – was the beginning of a geopolitical sensibility in colonial society. Geopolitics, a term in increasing use today, is not an ideology or a theory but a cast of mind. Originating in mid-nineteenth-century Germany, it was soon adopted by British and American strategists as a way of understanding the shifting tides of power around them and through history. Geopolitics challenges governments to think spatially about threats and opportunities: how their territories, topographies, waterways and seascapes make them either vulnerable or powerful. Strategy then challenges governments to make hard choices about how best to use limited resources to limit the weaknesses and exploit the advantages conferred by geography.

Thinking geopolitically tells us this about Australia: that we are difficult to invade, but relatively easy to coerce if hostile forces gain access to the islands to our north. Australia's major cities are clustered in the southeastern corner, requiring invading forces either to travel through thousands of kilometres of featureless desert or to traverse thousands of nautical miles of ocean. Both invasion options would be highly vulnerable to attack and would need overwhelming air and naval superiority to avoid the fate of all but a few successful amphibious invasions in history. Coercion, on the other hand, would be relatively straightforward. Australia's dependence on links with the rest of the world makes its shipping and air traffic vulnerable to attack or to blocking of the vital sea lanes and air corridors crossing the islands of Southeast Asia. Our fuel supplies alone are highly vulnerable to attack or blockade through Southeast Asia; even a month-long blockade would see supermarket shelves empty, medical supplies run out and the economy grind to a halt. And as the war in Ukraine shows, the means to attack shipping and air traffic are becoming cheaper, more readily available and more lethal.

This strategic reality alone should anchor Australia's attention to its immediate north. But there is another reason why Southeast Asia is of increasing importance to us. We are watching a new contest open up in world politics, the outcome of which will be profound. Its clearest articulation so far has been in the Trump administration's National Security Strategy, released in November 2025, which states, "The outsized influence of larger, richer and stronger nations is a timeless truth of international relations." Trump's deputy chief of staff, Stephen Miller, put it this way: "we live in a world, the real world, that is governed by strength, that is governed by force, that is governed by power. These are the iron laws of the world." These statements are not just hot air; they express what is actually happening: American actions in Venezuela and possibly Greenland, Russian actions in Ukraine, Chinese actions in the South China Sea.

These words and actions are a harbinger of a return of international relations to its default setting: a world in which the great powers claim mutually exclusive spheres of interest in which they can act with relative impunity. It seeks to overturn a way of organising global affairs that we have become used to, where every state, large or small, has (theoretically, at least) an equal right to exist, to determine its own domestic affairs and to a voice on international issues. This is a world that has accorded Australia a significant and activist voice in global affairs, and the reassurance that its rights as a state will be respected by others, large or small. The alternative mindset, ascendant in Washington, Beijing and Moscow, would see it enjoy no such rights, rather seeking constantly the forbearance of whichever great power claims its part of the world.

In the years ahead, the struggle between these two ways of organising the world – one hierarchic, one egalitarian – will become intense. Australia will not be a bystander. Nor will its northern neighbours, all of which are deeply committed to the sovereign equality of states. A world where powerful states are trying to usher their smaller neighbours into a zone in which the great power's will reigns supreme will require much greater solidarity among the smaller states that are trying to resist this outcome. Or, to put it another way, this is a world and a contest in which the dangers of diplomatic isolation will be acute.

Geopolitical reasoning tells us that what happens in Southeast Asia is of overwhelming importance to Australia's safety, prosperity and sovereignty – our capacity to determine our own values and way of life. There is no other priority that even comes close in existential importance. And yet Australian governments for well over a century have been distracted from this foundational geopolitical insight. Yes, we have regularly acknowledged the region to our immediate north in our defence documents, but these are like empty catechisms, ritually repeated and then forgotten. Understanding why this has happened, and what it will take to correct our strategic hyperopia, is arguably the most important question for Australia's future.

*

There are two main reasons for Australia's distractedness. The first is that for the past half-century, it has been other parts of Asia that have more insistently drawn our attention. The great economic boom that forged modern Australia was largely made in Northeast Asia. It started with the Korean War's demand for Australian commodities and continued with the reconstruction of the Japanese economy after World War II. Soon after, other industrialising Asian economies – South Korea, Taiwan, Hong Kong – showed a similar appetite for the minerals, energy and agricultural products that Australia produces so efficiently. The beginning of China's hunger for Australia's produce was evident by the late 1960s, even before we had formal diplomatic relations, when it became the second-largest customer for our wheat. More recently, Australia's economic attention has been dragged northwest towards India – and once more over Southeast Asia.

These remarkably lucrative economic links with the big industrialising economies of Asia touched off a countervailing concern – that we might be excluded from our region of greatest opportunity. Two variants of exclusion exercised Australian fears. One was a form of self-exclusion, through Australian society's failure to develop the cultural, linguistic and intellectual capabilities required to comprehend and engage with the booming societies of Asia. It was most clearly stated in a 1989 government-commissioned report, tellingly titled *Australia and the Northeast Asian Ascendancy*. In response, the government implemented a program of "Asia literacy" focusing on four languages: Japanese, Korean, Mandarin Chinese and Bahasa Indonesia – only one of four centred in Southeast Asia. The message was clearly received. In today's schools and universities, Japanese, Korean and Chinese language classes are viable; Indonesian classes are emptying and being shut down.

The other fear was of being shut out of an exclusive regional bloc, of the type that was taking shape in Europe. This led to a spree of geographic imaginings designed to define Australia into "its" region. The first such was the "Asia Pacific" and had an economic logic, describing Northeast Asia's booming industry, Southeast Asia's commodities and cheap labour, Australian minerals and energy, and America's voracious consumer markets. Most recently there has been the "Indo-Pacific," based on a security logic which sees the Indian and Pacific oceans' coastlines and waterways as a single strategic realm. All such concepts had the intent of embedding Australia in a broader region, but they have had the unintended effect of diffusing our diplomatic attention over a much wider zone than Southeast Asia.

The second cause of our distractedness has been our alliance commitments. Modern Australia has only ever known a world in which an English-speaking great power, with which it shares political values and cultural familiarity, has been globally dominant. Its foreign policy imperative for over two centuries has been to form as close as possible a security partnership with that dominant power, and to help defend its global dominance. The instinct to cleave ever more closely to first the British Empire and then the United States with the ANZUS alliance has distracted Australian governments from maintaining a laser focus on our immediate region.

By co-opting a great power to our defence, Australian governments have committed to delivering on that power's global strategy, rather than focusing on our own local imperatives. The history of our military commitments and diplomacy reveals this clearly. The first Australian troops committed abroad defended the British Empire in Sudan and South Africa and secured British interests in China against the Boxer Rebellion. Our first action in World War I was to seize German territories in New Guinea and Samoa, but thereafter Australia spent blood and treasure to defend British power in Europe and the Middle East. As the Japanese swept through Southeast Asia and Melanesia in World War II, Australian forces were in the Middle East fighting to defend British interests. To Winston Churchill's ire, as we have seen, Prime Minister John Curtin insisted Australian troops be brought back to our region to meet the Japanese challenge. Our commitments during the Cold War were initially to help the United States and UK defend the Middle East, before US and British attention – and our own – was drawn back to the Korean Peninsula and Southeast Asia by the threat of communism. Our largest engagements this century have been to Afghanistan and Iraq – once again in support of American strategy.

The luxury of always having the world's most powerful country in our corner has inevitably shaped how Australians see the world. Because of their deep investment in the continued dominance of their ally, Australian policy-makers have come to share its perspective on threats and interests. British rivalry with Russia in Central Asia in the nineteenth century caused such apprehension in Australia that the colony of New South Wales built Fort Denison in Sydney Harbour to deter the Russian navy. There was no evidence that Russia had the capability or intent to attack Australia. British confrontations with France and Germany before World War I led to widespread fear of French and German bases in the Pacific, motivating the colony of Queensland to make a farcical attempt to annex New Guinea on behalf of the Crown in 1883. During the Cold War, Canberra willingly subscribed to US conceptions of a monolithic communist movement, adapting its thinking and commitments to evolving American strategies of containment. The Whitlam government's brief departure from US preferences, simultaneously recognising the People's Republic of China, North Vietnam and North Korea in 1973, led to deep recriminations within the alliance and within the Australian government; no successor has contemplated diverging from US strategy since. After the Cold War, Canberra has seamlessly adapted its foreign and defence policies to follow the American lead, enthusiastically signing up to fight the War on Terror and transform the Middle East. Our foreign and defence policy has a heliocentric quality: it is consistently shaped by the perceptions and strategies of our great ally.

In consequence, Australia has serially committed to objectives that are completely beyond its capabilities to deliver. If strategy is the discipline of matching objectives with available means, Australian governments have consistently failed to develop that discipline. Their logic has been that by engaging the capabilities of the most powerful state on Earth, Australia vastly increases its means and so can afford to have more expansive objectives. The problem with this logic is that the objectives are not Australia's to choose, but its ally's; as we'll see, this risks undermining Australia's vital interests when its ally acts in ways that alienate important neighbours and partners. America's strategic failures are mounting, from its attempts at democratising the Middle East, to building a viable Afghanistan, to its campaign to prevent nuclear proliferation. The recently launched campaign to assert US supremacy in the Western Hemisphere and exclude other powers has strategic failure written all over it. Each failure diminishes the reputation, authority and power of the United States, and emboldens those powers that want to challenge the global order Australia has found so comforting. And being heliocentric in our thinking becomes especially problematic when our major ally lurches towards an attitude to international relations that is actively harmful to our basic interests, sovereign equality and voice in international affairs.

*

The costs of Australia's serial distraction from its own geopolitical imperatives have been masked by the fact that maritime Southeast Asia has been peaceful, focused on economic development and benignly disposed towards Australia since 1966. Over that time, following the fall of President Sukarno in Indonesia, governments in Canberra have come to take the stability and pragmatism of our northern neighbours for granted. The cavalier way Australia has treated Indonesia, from boat tow-backs to leading an intervention in East Timor, show how complacent we have become about the non-problematic nature of Southeast Asia.

Australia has been blessed by a serendipitous convergence of interests with its Southeast Asian neighbours. They have benefited just as much as we have from the benign trading and investment environment that developed around the Pacific Rim in the 1980s and 1990s. Southeast Asian states sublimated their rivalries and disagreements into regional rituals of consultation and consensus, and accepted American primacy. In such a stable and pragmatic neighbourhood, Australian foreign policy seldom needed to exert diplomatic ambition or initiative. Maintaining cordial relations, attending regional consultations and respecting regional norms appeared to be all that was required.

We have forgotten just how different the picture was in the decade before Sukarno was toppled in 1965. The Indonesian president, fired by the independence struggle against the Dutch, had campaigned for *Indonesia Raya* – greater Indonesia – which included absorbing West Irian and the Malayan territories of Sarawak, Sabah and Singapore. Increasingly anti-Western in tone, Sukarno saw Western colonialist conspiracy everywhere. He began to promote an axis with Mao's China and Kim Il Sung's North Korea, claiming leadership of a revolutionary coalition of the developing against the developed world. The alarm in Canberra was justifiably profound. Australia campaigned hard against the Indonesian claim to what would become West Papua. Australian troops were dispatched to Malaya to defend its sovereignty against Indonesian incursions, and Australia bought a state-of-the-art fleet of F-111 fighter bombers, specifically chosen because they would be able to attack Indonesian territory from northern Australia in the event of hostilities.

But luck intervened in three forms for Australia. First, a military coup toppled Sukarno and brought the Western-leaning General Suharto to power. The second element of our geopolitical luck was that for almost four decades after the normalisation of US–China ties in the 1970s, great-power competition reduced markedly in Southeast Asia. With China internally focused, US supremacy in Southeast Asia was uncontested. The third piece of luck was the forging of a regional association among Southeast Asian states that would allow them to concentrate on developing their own economies and societies. For the forty years after the end of the Vietnam War, Australia appeared to live in a postmodern region of peace and prosperity, unchallenged by the tensions that confronted other states. It seemed geopolitics had gone to sleep.

Over time, we have become accustomed to a Micawberian view of Southeast Asia, assuming that despite all the colour and movement of election campaigns and regional summitry, somehow everything will always turn out for the best. But if history teaches us anything, it is the folly of assuming that international affairs is a realm of predictability and continuity. Escalating great-power rivalry has returned to Southeast Asia. Within the region, arms spending has increased, as have tensions and even conflict between some of its states. Political volatility is also rising, making the sudden transformation of one or several of the archipelagic states to our north by no means remote.

The tides are moving against Australia's interests in subtle and largely unnoticed ways. The advantages that gave Australia significance and credibility in Southeast Asia – our wealth and technological sophistication, our military capabilities and our alliance with the United States – no longer command such respect. Southeast Asia's own development makes Australia's wealth and technology less significant by the year and is eroding Australia's military edge, while America's commitments and credibility in Southeast Asia appear increasingly thin. Meanwhile, Canberra's recent and total focus on countering China's rise is drawing it further and further from the perceptions and priorities of our neighbours.

We therefore confront the increasingly dangerous consequences of ignoring our geopolitical imperatives for so long. Our inattention to how Southeast Asia is constituted, the factors and forces that drive its political evolution, impedes our ability to understand just how profoundly dangerous a situation this is.

WITHOUT A MAP

Most Australians view Southeast Asia not as a crucible of competition but as an extended hedonistic playground. Every week, budget airlines deliver thousands of Australian pleasure-seekers to the beaches of Bali, Phuket, Langkawi and Cebu, transforming Southeast Asia's tropical islands into copies of Australia's leisure centres: Noosa, Bondi, Burleigh, Torquay. The same airlines return to Australia full of tourists with Bin Tang singlets, tattoos, braided hair and glowing tans, but little the wiser about the countries and cultures they have just visited. Indeed, the more favoured resorts are those that most hermetically seal off the great Australian hedonism from the surrounding society and culture. Few would comprehend how crucial these sun-kissed islands are to the future security, prosperity and international influence of their country.

Australians' inattentiveness to their northern neighbours is shared by their governments. Despite regular homilies on the importance of those islands to its north, Australia has never drawn a coherent map of its interests in Southeast Asia. In all the thousands of pages of white papers, planning documents, strategic reviews, ministerial speeches and statements churned out of Canberra since the end of World War II, one might search in vain for a clear account of what is most important to Australia in managing relations with its Southeast Asian neighbours. From 1946, regular assessments were made about types of threats Australia faced in the region, and against which Australia needed to be prepared. These are overwhelmingly reactive, responding to threats as they arise rather than developing a long-term and deliberate stance of calibrated engagement. Where broad statements of commitment were made, such as bolstering neighbouring countries' resilience against communist subversion, or supporting their stability and development, they could equally be applied to any other country or region with which Australia had significant ties.

Most consistently, and particularly in the last half-century, there is a general yearning for acceptance, largely reacting to a hidden fear that Australia will be rejected by its northern neighbours and become ever more isolated.

The synonyms have proliferated over the years – engagement, enmeshment, integration – but the fear remains constant. The general focus on building acceptance has the advantage of looking purposeful while the ultimate objectives and rationales of our diplomacy remain unclear. Mostly one finds bromides about the importance of the region or a particular country, and a laundry list of all the initiatives Canberra is pursuing to secure positive relations with its northern neighbours – a long line of security agreements, strategic partnerships and trade agreements.

There is no clearer evidence of the tendency to look over Southeast Asia to more compelling economic and strategic interests than in Australia's three Foreign Policy White Papers. The 1997 White Paper lists four countries "which most substantially engage Australia's interests": the United States, Japan, China and Indonesia. The "other ASEAN states" are relegated to a secondary tier. The 2003 White Paper adds the Republic of Korea to the front rank. The 2016 White Paper elevates the United States and China to the front rank and then pledges to "lift the ambition of our engagement with major Indo-Pacific democracies": Japan, Indonesia, India and Korea. Southeast Asia is once again on the next tier down.

In these documents and many others, Australia's strategists have struggled with the central paradox of Australia's location. Southeast Asia is our region of primary geopolitical interest, the place where developments can most profoundly affect our security and diplomatic voice (and have done so), but it also sits within a broader strategic realm, in which rivalries, interdependences and solidarities with larger powers in Northeast Asia and potentially South Asia have a significant impact on what happens closer to home. Since World War II, Canberra's response to this paradox has been to try to influence broader dynamics, sometimes through its US alliance, sometimes through regional institutions, as a way of advancing its preferences in Southeast Asia. This was the rationale behind Australia's strong advocacy of the Asia-Pacific Economic Cooperation (APEC), the ASEAN Regional Forum and the broader East Asia Summit, and, more recently, the Quadrilateral Security Dialogue ("the Quad").

What is becoming clear, however, is that Australia's contributions to shaping these broader dynamics in Northeast and South Asia were at best slight and are steadily decreasing in impact. The regional institutions we championed in the past have less and less purchase on the calculations and possibilities of the great powers, while our alliance with America has given us little leverage in shaping US policy towards Southeast Asia. In the world of Donald Trump, Australia's role in steeling American resolve to play a stabilising role in Asia is a fast-perishing asset. To think that in 2026 Canberra has any influence on the trajectory of US–China relations, Japan–China dynamics or China–India rivalries and alignments – or on any of their intentions relating to Southeast Asia – is utterly fanciful. Consequently, Australia needs to recognise that its interests in its region of primary strategic priority have to be pursued primarily in Southeast Asia, and only secondarily in Northeast Asia or South Asia or the broader Indo-Pacific. To do that, it must refocus its attention on its nearer north.

A strategic map would begin with a set of questions. What are Southeast Asia's dynamics of solidarity and faultlines of tension? Which states, islands and waterways are most important to Australia, and why? Which issues and interests align Australia with particular countries, and which are likely to lead to serious friction and disagreement? How do Southeast Asia's governments view Australia, and how could Australia better position itself in regional calculations? Most importantly, what are Australia's interests in the region, and what are the most effective ways to work with existing predispositions and rivalries to secure them? Such a detailed map requires a double understanding: of what Australia's interests are in the region, and of the local factors that will assist or hinder their achievement.

This requires an effort in geopolitical empathy, seeking to comprehend how the countries of Southeast Asia understand themselves and the world around them. It involves taking into account the rich history of the region and its societies, the ethnic and religious mosaics this history has woven, past and future economic advantages and dependencies, as well as contemporary political dynamics. Geopolitical empathy is necessary to avoid a form of the strategic ethnocentrism that plagues Anglophone countries, making us assume that other countries think of their national interests in the same way we do. Understanding the region intimately needs to precede a hardheaded process of strategic calculation, determining which parts of the region are more important to Australia, based on a clear appreciation of Australia's own interests.

*

Geography and history have been the most powerful shapers of the societies of Southeast Asia. Most of its 3000 islands sit atop the Sunda Shelf, the shallowness of which brings a rare calm to the seas between the islands. This maritime domain, plus the horticultural and mineral richness of these islands, the regularity of the winds and monsoons, and their position between the great civilisations of India and China combined to make this the most vigorous trading region on Earth for centuries before the arrival of the first Europeans. Other ports grew along the great rivers flowing into the Sunda Sea from the Asian continent or close to narrow straits, drawing coastal societies into a rich maritime trading world. The trade winds brought outside influences – Sanskrit and political and religious doctrines from India; wealth, literature and philosophy from China; Islam from Arabia via the subcontinent. This trading history has left these island and coastal societies with complex tapestries of ethnic and religious communities and a compulsive outward-looking focus.

The societies of the region also developed a strong sense of distinctiveness. Despite their borrowings from Indian and Chinese civilisations, they refused to be subsumed by them, adapting what they borrowed to local conditions. As they became incorporated into European empires, they were similarly resistant to Western cultural and religious dogmas; with the exception of the Philippines, there was no widespread conversion of Malay societies to Christianity. Vietnamese, Filipinos and Indonesians proved themselves repeatedly willing to fight for their independence from external rulers. As anti-colonial movements at times sustained dreams of pan-Asian solidarity, Southeast Asian resistance leaders refused to be subsumed into a broader movement led by larger and more assertive countries. This sense of distinctiveness has remained and at times manifested in anxiety among the Malay populations of Indonesia, Malaysia, Brunei and Singapore that they will be surpassed or suppressed by outside influences – whether it be external powers or internal migrant communities. This can give the internal and external politics of Southeast Asian states a particular combustibility.

Decolonisation came quickly to Southeast Asia, with the European and American empires first pushed aside by the Japanese and then thrown off by local resistance movements. The task of forging national unity was especially daunting in island Southeast Asia, with its states divided among hundreds or thousands of islands and diverse ethnic groups and religions. Two decades of revolt and instability built among regional governments a sense of shared vulnerability – which only deepened as Southeast Asia became the second front of the Cold War, the crucible of a shadow conflict between the United States, the Soviet Union and communist China. Following so soon on the heels of colonialism, these experiences bred a deep aversion among Southeast Asians to being used by outside powers for their interests, or being marginalised by big countries with large regional designs. The island states also nurture a sense of archipelagic insecurity – an awareness that the task of defending themselves is out of all proportion to the resources they can deploy. Their security must flow primarily from non-military means, which makes solidarity and diplomatic balancing their first and only line of defence.

Perhaps the strongest expression of postcolonial Southeast Asia's refusal to be entangled in power politics occurred in 1955 in Bandung, in the highlands east of Jakarta, when Asian and African states gathered in a movement of "non-alignment" with either of the superpowers. Out of the experience of mutual vulnerability and sensitivity to being caught up in outside power games grew a solidarity among Southeast Asia's non-communist states, articulated at Bangkok in August 1967 with the formation of the Association of Southeast Asian Nations, or ASEAN. It remains by a long distance the most successful regional organisation created by former colonies. But solidarity within the grouping is limited by a prickly insistence on sovereignty. Collective undertakings are difficult to achieve and often of little importance because of members' insistence that all decisions must be unanimous. Yet, at the same time, Southeast Asian diplomacy repeatedly shows that states incorporate a sense of the regional interest, along with their specific national interests, in how they deal with the world.

By the 1970s, Southeast Asia became an economic hinterland for the surging postwar Japanese economy, which had been shut out of mainland Asia by communist regimes in China, North Korea, Vietnam, Laos and Cambodia. That the Southeast Asian states willingly embraced Japanese aid and development so soon after being brutally occupied by Japan demonstrates their outward-focused pragmatism and focus on development. Stability, sovereignty and development emerged as the leitmotifs of the new states of Southeast Asia, forging a sense of solidarity among them. Hyper-aware that theirs is a region prey to great-power rivalries, Southeast Asian states are vigorous in asserting their agency. The instinct to non-alignment with outside powers articulated at Bandung remains strong. Although it hasn't stopped states such as the Philippines, Thailand and Vietnam forming alliances with one or other of the superpowers, it has limited these alliances' scope and depth to the point where they have unravelled quickly as the original motivating threat declined. In the region's recent history, tight alignments have brought bloodshed and restricted economic development. They can also threaten to upset often tense internal and regional ethnic balances. A delicate equilibrium is maintained within the region: if one or more states aligns with external powers, the others seek to balance and offset these alignments. The repeated preference for not aligning collectively is Southeast Asia's ultimate act of agency, sovereignty and autonomy.

*

At the geopolitical heart of Southeast Asia, its political and strategic centre of gravity, are the islands of Java, Borneo, Sumatra and Singapore, plus the Malay Peninsula, a long, thin land bridge that extends from the Asian mainland down into the heart of the archipelago. These islands and peninsula, plus Australia, form a terrestrial barrier between the Indian and Pacific oceans, making the narrow straits between them the most strategically important waterways of the twenty-first century. They also host the bulk of the region's population, and a large proportion of its agricultural production, industrial capability and wealth.

Three of the four states that control these islands and peninsula – Indonesia, Malaysia and Singapore – form the strategic core of Southeast Asia. Indonesia's size makes it the region's *primus inter pares*, although it has always struggled to assert itself and have its leadership acknowledged by its neighbours. Its size and dispersed geography make it predominantly introspective and highly sensitive to its internal cohesion. Its prolonged anti-colonial struggle gives Indonesians a sense of pride, an inflamed sensitivity to issues of sovereignty, and a deep commitment to non-alignment and postcolonial solidarity. Malaysia straddles the peninsula and the island of Borneo, where two of its states sit. Singapore has neither the size nor scale of its two neighbours, but its geographic position, economic dynamism and diplomatic adroitness give it a pivotal role in the region.

The triangular relationship between Indonesia, Malaysia and Singapore creates a nucleus of tension and interdependence around which the rest of the region revolves. It involves intense mutual suspicion, ethnically driven economic and diplomatic rivalry, and deep economic and infrastructural integration. Indonesia and Malaysia combine a shared history of pan-Malay consciousness and solidarity with an intense rivalry over which society represents authentic "Malay-ness," as they compete for leadership in Southeast Asia, the Global South and the Muslim world. The rivalry between Indonesia and Malaysia erupted into open hostility soon after Malaya's independence, when Jakarta labelled the new state a colonialist construct and sent special forces to attack its territory, which Australia contributed forces to defend. Indonesia and Malaysia are both majority Malay states that host significant ethnic Chinese minorities, whose wealth and business acumen stimulate anxieties among the majority that they will be eclipsed politically and economically. Both countries have seen deadly ethnic riots and pogroms since independence, and these tensions led to the expulsion of ethnic Chinese-majority Singapore from the Malayan Federation in 1965. As a small, Chinese-majority state between two much larger Malay-majority neighbours, Singapore is acutely sensitive to any signs of a pan-Malay compact between Indonesia and Malaysia and is quietly contented when fraternal rivalries bubble to the surface.

Singapore sits between Indonesia and Malaysia as an embodiment of their anxieties: a wealthy, successful majority-ethnic-Chinese state with a disempowered Malay minority. The tensions that led to Malaysia and Singapore's separation are never far from the surface. Each state accuses the other – justifiably – of being an ethno-chauvinist regime, with Malaysia practising positive discrimination in favour of its Malay citizens, while Singapore protects its status as a majority-Chinese and Chinese-led state. Ethnic rivalry translates into economic competition, with development being interpreted as evidence of the superiority of the dominant culture in each state. Singapore's more advanced level of economic and technological development pushes the buttons of deep-seated Malay insecurities in its two neighbours. The negative stereotypes are mutual. Indonesians tend to see Singapore as self-interested and extractive of Indonesia's wealth. They too are suspicious of Singapore's assertive Chinese-ness, believing that the island state courts the loyalties of Indonesia's own Chinese minority. Jakarta has long suspected Singapore of willingly hosting corrupt Indonesian businesspeople and using Chinese trading networks to extract wealth from Indonesia.

The three countries are heavily interdependent and crowded into close proximity, making their frequent disputes potentially explosive. Malaysia, for instance, has regularly threatened to cut off Singapore's supply of water, an act that would almost certainly be interpreted by the city-state as an existential threat. The depth of mutual insecurity between these three states and the intensity of their diplomatic rivalry create a dynamism that drives broader regional imperatives and possibilities. No significant regional initiative can succeed if two of the three oppose it, but the opposition of one can be neutralised by cultivating the other two. Their combined approach to managing the great powers – Indonesia's and Malaysia's doctrinaire non-alignment balanced by Singapore's pragmatic multiple engagement – creates the diplomatic centre of gravity for the region.

Thailand, the Philippines and Vietnam form the next layer of geopolitical significance in Southeast Asia. Together they add close to 300 million people and more than US$1.5 trillion in GDP to ASEAN. But they are religiously, culturally and ideologically remote from the Malay–Chinese dynamics of Indonesia, Malaysia and Singapore. Vietnam is a staunchly communist regime in an organisation once avowedly anti-communist, while Thailand and the Philippines are unstable democracies, prone to cycles of popular protest and military rule at unpredictable intervals. They are also the countries that have been most willing to ally with outside powers – Thailand and the Philippines as treaty allies of the United States, and Vietnam as an ally of communist China and the Soviet Union during the Cold War. These alliances have never been deep, though, waxing and waning with changes in strategic context.

There are also complex relations between these second-tier states. Thailand and Vietnam were strategic rivals during the Cold War and continue to watch each other's influence on the buffer states of Cambodia and Laos. The Philippines and Vietnam have been the most willing to challenge China's claims to the South China Sea, but neither has been able to rally the core states or ASEAN as a whole behind their confrontations with Beijing. More generally, although the three second-tier states bring heft to ASEAN, they have rarely been able to lead the region. During their democratic phases, Bangkok and Manila have advocated the modernisation of regional institutions and norms, such as mutual non-interference and higher environmental and human rights standards. On these issues, as on the South China Sea, second-tier states struggle to enlist the more conservative core states in support of their initiatives.

The third geopolitical tier of Southeast Asia consists of Myanmar, Cambodia and Laos. These are ASEAN's most recent members, and the least integrated. Politically, they are the most problematic: Laos is communist,

Cambodia an authoritarian state, and Myanmar a military junta engaged in a vicious war with its own people. Cambodia has an ongoing border dispute with Thailand, which has also come to blows with Myanmar. Myanmar's brutal treatment of its Muslim Rohingya minority has roused the ire of Muslim-majority Indonesia and Malaysia. Due to their international isolation and close proximity to China, all three states are particularly prone to Beijing's influence and see ASEAN membership as a way of balancing their dependence on Beijing. China has been able to use its influence on Cambodia to prevent ASEAN Summit communiqués from mentioning the territorial disputes in the South China Sea, raising fears that Beijing seeks to fracture ASEAN. However, the peripheral role the third-tier states play in regional geopolitics suggests these fears may be overstated.

These dynamics and tiers of influence and significance are nowhere articulated. You would search in vain to find them written in ASEAN agreements or communiqués, or hear them uttered aloud in meeting rooms or at conferences. The region's symbolism is heavy on egalitarianism, solidarity and forbearance. Where they do become evident is on close observation of what Southeast Asian states do and don't do; which initiatives they support and which they oppose; which leaders articulate what the region eventually supports, and which leaders' suggestions are politely noted and then ignored.

*

Southeast Asia's states share an acute awareness of their region's geopolitical importance, and their individual and collective vulnerabilities to great-power rivalry and domination. Relatively recent memories of colonisation, Cold War conflict and great-power intervention mean that these sensitivities are intense and ever-present. One of the most powerful drivers of solidarity within ASEAN has been the desire not to give a powerful state any pretext to step in to restore regional order.

Over eight decades, these states have developed different ways of avoiding undue attention from their powerful neighbours. The original formula was non-alignment, championed by Indonesia at Bandung in 1955, advocating for solidarity among former colonies in refusing to align with either side in the Cold War. Over time, Indonesia and Malaysia have been the strongest and most consistent advocates of non-alignment, while Thailand, the Philippines and Singapore have rejected this approach and opted to align with the United States. Another approach was to attempt to commit outside powers to the ASEAN norms of sovereign equality, non-intervention and the non-use of force through a succession of initiatives with bewildering acronyms: the Zone of Peace, Freedom and Neutrality (ZOPFAN); the Southeast Asia Nuclear Weapons Free Zone (SEANWFZ); and the Treaty on Amity and Cooperation (TAC). Each has had little success in binding outside powers to the region's preferred behaviours. The third approach has been to encourage the United States to play a stabilising but benignly neglectful role, anchored by security partnerships with the Philippines, Thailand and Singapore and lower-level cooperation with Indonesia, Malaysia and Brunei.

A fourth approach to avoiding damaging competition or intervention has been labelled "omni-balancing," or, to use the words of Indonesia's President Prabowo, being "friends to all, and enemies to none." This strategy aims to engage all interested great powers, providing individual states in the region with alternatives if one great power tries to coerce or capture their allegiance, and a collective balance among rivals to ensure that no individual power can unilaterally dominate. It is a plan that works better in theory than in practice. China has much greater capacity, proximity and incentive to build influence in Southeast Asia than any other outside power. The United States has decreasing incentives and capabilities, relative to China's. Other contenders, such as India and Japan, lack the compelling motivation or legitimacy, respectively, to play a serious stabilising role. The geopolitics of the broader region around Southeast Asia are shifting inexorably, creating stark choices for its countries and its southern neighbour, Australia, about how to achieve, in Foreign Minister Penny Wong's striking phrase, "a strategic equilibrium" in which "no country dominates, and no country is dominated." Understanding these larger power dynamics is essential to understanding the scale of the challenge to our immediate north.

SPHERE OF DEFERENCE

When President Xi Jinping stood to address the Indonesian parliament on 2 October 2013, few would have realised he was announcing an epochal change in Chinese strategy. Buried among bland recitations of proverbs and declarations of eternal friendship between China and Indonesia was a seemingly innocuous statement: "Southeast Asia has since ancient times been an important hub along the ancient maritime Silk Road … [China will] vigorously develop maritime partnership[s] in a joint effort to build the Maritime Silk Road of the twenty-first century." This statement, along with Xi's promise to build a new "Silk Road Economic Belt" a month earlier, in Astana, Kazakhstan, signalled a new assertiveness in Beijing's approach to Asia and the world.

Xi's predecessors Jiang Zemin and Deng Xiaoping had insisted on a non-threatening, non-disruptive stance to foreign relations, with China "hiding its strength and biding its time" to reassure neighbours that its rise was benign. Now, just half a year into his presidency, Xi had inaugurated a frenetic international program, including what would come to be known as the Belt and Road Initiative (BRI), a new Asian Infrastructure Investment Bank (AIIB), announced in the same speech to the Indonesian parliament, and a "Community of Common Destiny" between China and its neighbours in Asia. More ominously, China began large-scale dredging and land reclamation operations across seven reefs in the South China Sea, in waters claimed by Vietnam and the Philippines under the Law of the Sea. By 2016 over 3000 acres of new land had been created, some of which hosted advanced military facilities such as ports, runways and missile batteries, despite Xi's earlier promises that the islands would not be militarised. The days of hiding and biding were over.

Xi's speech in Jakarta returned several times to the long, historical connections between China and the region it traditionally referred to as *Nanyang* – the South Sea. To many of those listening in that cavernous parliament there were unsettling portents behind the bromides of friendship and mutual benefit. For centuries, regimes that have ruled China have looked at the region to the south as a political and economic hinterland. Southeast Asia was both a source of and a conduit for luxury goods – spices, textiles, exotic woods and foods, precious metals – that were in high demand among Chinese elites. Imperial China's preferences for how it obtained these goods, sometimes welcoming traders to its ports, sometimes designating a Southeast Asian port as its sole source of supply, played a major role in the rise and fall of Southeast Asian empires in the centuries before the arrival of Europeans. The China trade could make Southeast Asian rajas and their ports rich and powerful; what the Chinese demanded in return was the rajas' acknowledgement of the superiority of China's civilisation. Imperial China's international relations were based on the extraction of tribute – the symbolic deference to their cultural superiority – in return for access to the lucrative Chinese market.

Modern China inherited this centuries-long understanding of Southeast Asia as a hinterland. The arrival of the Europeans had changed China's world utterly but had not dislodged its particular focus on the territories and islands to its south. These were places where trade and investment had been long seeded, where thousands of Chinese people had relocated, both voluntarily and by necessity. As modern China succumbed to civil war between nationalist and communist forces, both sides saw Southeast Asia as a region of political danger and opportunity. Overseas Chinese populations could be a source of support or succour to opponents, and so both sides began cultivating and mobilising Southeast Asian Chinese communities – in turn, greatly alarming their majority-Malay neighbours. The sense that ethnic Chinese living beyond China's borders are still part of the nation, potential supporters or subverters of the regime, to be either protected or suppressed, continued even after the Chinese Communist Party (CCP) took power. Today, it is estimated that 30 million people of Chinese descent live in Southeast Asia – or 70 per cent of all ethnic Chinese living outside China.

No other region comes close to Southeast Asia in the opportunities and potential threats it presents to the fast-rising behemoth that is today's

China. The region's population, wealth and economic dynamism offer outlets and growth potential to a Chinese economy throttled by rising costs and overcapacity. There are strategic vulnerabilities and benefits to consider too. Island Southeast Asia sits as an immovable rampart between the Indian and Pacific oceans. In unfriendly hands, this archipelago is a potential chokepoint for the vital energy supplies from the Gulf oilfields that sustain China's economy and society. In friendly hands, it can potentially host ports and bases that allow the People's Liberation Army, Navy and Airforce to range freely across two of the world's largest oceans and Asia's long and wealthy coastline. With a population of 700 million and combined GDP of almost $4 trillion, a Southeast Asia tightly integrated with China – economically, politically, technologically – would be a major adjunct to China's wealth and strength, and a major loss of markets, bases and access to China's rivals. A Southeast Asia willing to align with China would send a strong signal to other developing regions across Asia, Africa and Latin America that these pragmatic, development-minded, post-colonial states feel able to trust Beijing's pledges not to act like an exploitative, judgemental, Western great power.

Such is the scale of opportunity and potential vulnerability that it is no exaggeration to say that Southeast Asia is pivotal to China's prospects of becoming a truly global great power. China's leaders refer to Southeast Asia as part of their *zhoubian* (periphery), similar to Russia's concept of its "near abroad." A China with Southeast Asia as its economic, political and strategic adjunct will have the economic heft, regime legitimacy and geographic advantages to steadily scale up its global influence for the rest of the century. On the other hand, if Beijing is unable to secure unchallenged primacy in Southeast Asia, it will remain regionally bound, lacking the confidence, access and legitimacy to exert genuinely global influence. A Southeast Asia that is resistant to China's will means continued uncertainty for Beijing about the security of its energy flows, and evidence that its closest neighbours mistrust its pledges to be a different type of great power. A Southeast Asia beyond China's sway is a region potentially able to host forces hostile to its security and subversive of its political system – a region potentially able to be caught up in a rival economic bloc intended to exclude and contain China. As in no other region, Southeast Asia is where the prospects, nature and implications of China's global power will become manifest.

*

So critical is Southeast Asia to China's fortunes that it has called forth an impulse common to rising great powers: the desire to construct a sphere of interest. It is an urge that originates in a paradox all too common in rising leviathans: as they become richer and stronger, they feel ever more vulnerable – a pathology that feeds their unquenchable thirst for power. When their vulnerabilities are acutely identified in territories close to their borders, their urge is to extend their sway in order to eliminate those liabilities. So it was the misfortune of the low countries – today's Belgium and the Netherlands – that both a rising England and a rising France saw them as a potential platform from which one waxing power could attack the other from the seventeenth to the twentieth centuries. Paris and London were unable to resist meddling in these restive provinces. As the United States began to coalesce and flex its newfound capacities in the early nineteenth century, President James Monroe issued his famous proclamation warning European powers against dabbling in the rivalries in the Americas. What followed was a long series of American interventions in its southern neighbours' affairs that continues to this day, as the Trump administration asserts the rights to exclusive influence in the Western Hemisphere. The Soviet Union designated Eastern Europe its inviolable sphere of interest after World War II, just as post-Soviet Russia has revived its forceful claims to its "near abroad" in Ukraine, Georgia, Moldova, Belarus and perhaps the Baltic states.

Spheres of interest come in different forms and with different levels of completeness. If the great power's threat assessments coincide with those of its neighbours – say, a common fear of terrorism – the sphere of interest can be benign and relatively consensual. Where their perceptions are at odds – as with Soviet fears of Western capitalism and democracy and Eastern

Europeans' yearning for these – the sphere can be coercive and totalising. Generally, a great power's fears about its near abroad focus on excluding peer competitors from gaining a foothold and preventing these neighbouring territories from nurturing movements that could undermine its legitimacy or stability.

China's primary concern is the continued rule of the CCP; all other interests are subordinated to regime security. It fears economic instability and political opposition, and yearns for "national reunification" with Taiwan, because of what they mean for the legitimacy of the Communist Party. And so what Beijing fears most in its near abroad in Southeast Asia are developments that will weaken the CCP's grip on power. It fears an entrenched ongoing American presence in Southeast Asia because it sees the goal of US foreign policy as being to overthrow the communist regime in China. Beijing is also sensitive to criticism from within Southeast Asian societies, which it worries will give succour to opponents at home. Its main urge, then, is to control developments that could undermine Communist Party rule. In ways reminiscent of imperial China's attitude to Southeast Asia, Beijing seeks a "Sphere of Deference," in which Southeast Asian states agree to abide by Beijing's wishes in both domestic and foreign policy, where these are deemed by China to affect its regime security.

*

China's approach to building a Sphere of Deference to its south has been multi-pronged. Its most potent asset is its surging economy. The three wellsprings of the CCP's pursuit of economic growth and technological dominance are a sense of humiliation at the hands of European, American and Japanese imperialists; apprehension that the West will seek to frustrate China's rise; and a deep-seated, never-relinquished, Marxist economic determinism. The result is a single-minded national will to power rarely seen before in global affairs. The scale and pace of China's economic rise has unleashed tidal forces across the world economy, affecting its closest neighbours first and most profoundly. China has become the foremost trading partner of every Southeast Asian economy, with more Chinese exports going to the region than to either the United States or Europe since 2023. Currently, around one-third of Southeast Asia's imports are from China. A closer look shows that economies across Southeast Asia have become deeply embedded in Chinese manufacturing supply chains: much of what Southeast Asia imports from China are component parts for goods that are assembled and exported to other markets. But they are also recipients of finished Chinese manufactures, having seen an 18 per cent increase in Chinese exports to the region after Trump's "Liberation Day" tariffs reduced Chinese companies' access to the US market.

The states of Southeast Asia share many of China's motivations for economic development. Becoming part of the East Asian economic miracle speaks to post-colonial yearnings for evidence of national worth, while providing a sense of national resilience and independence. These motivations were reinforced in 1997, when the region succumbed to a financial crisis that gutted the Indonesian, Thai, Malaysian and Philippines economies, leading to serious unrest in all. Beijing's rapid economic ascent and new forms of outreach have facilitated the willing integration of China's economy with those of its southern neighbours. Beijing couches these initiatives as "South–South cooperation" and mutual benefit, but few doubt that economic integration is building it leverage over its southern neighbours. As Southeast Asians have watched Beijing's campaigns of economic coercion against Japan, Korea, the Philippines and Australia in recent years, there are clear signs of nervousness about what this bargain could mean. Annual surveys conducted by the National University of Singapore's Yusof Ishak Institute show that as China's influence in the region has increased, Southeast Asians' trust in its intentions has been falling steadily.

The CCP's thoroughly Marxist reading of history creates a confidence that economic dominance will inevitably lead to overall dominance. Xi's language during meetings with regional leaders is peppered with admonitions to assert "strategic autonomy [from the US]," "democratise international relations" and build a "Community of Shared Future" between China and

Southeast Asia. China's new regionalism, driven by frenetic diplomatic summitry, large investments in area studies at Chinese universities, the education of thousands of Southeast Asian students on full scholarships at Chinese universities and provision of CCP-curated media content and channels to the region, represents a comprehensive attempt to win hearts and minds. Its "Digital Silk Road" initiative has resulted in Chinese provision of 4G and 5G telecommunications infrastructure, data centres and e-commerce platforms across all Southeast Asian countries. In classic sphere-of-influence behaviour, Beijing clearly aims to exclude external powers – the United States, in particular – from the affairs of Southeast Asia. In 2014, Xi called "for the people of Asia to run the affairs of Asia, solve the problems of Asia, and uphold the security of Asia."

In a region sensitive to threats to stability, China has also offered security cooperation. Beijing has established annual defence and foreign policy dialogues with Vietnam, Indonesia and Cambodia, and become a significant supplier of military equipment to Thailand, Myanmar and Malaysia. Its "Global Security Initiative" program has led to more comprehensive security partnerships with Vietnam, Malaysia, Thailand, Myanmar, Cambodia and Laos. To combat the growing challenge of transnational crime, particularly in mainland Southeast Asia, Beijing has successfully developed "inside-out" security partnerships, involving joint policing, shared data centres and the export of surveillance technologies.

But China's influence in Southeast Asia is not all blandishments and offers of "win-win cooperation." To the fishermen and coastguards of the Philippines, Beijing's prerogatives have a coercive and potentially deadly edge. In the waters within the Philippines' exclusive economic zone, China Coast Guard ships have repeatedly attacked fishing and naval vessels, using a range of tactics such as swarming, ramming and boarding, as well as using water cannons, military lasers and sonic weapons. Clashes have also occurred between Chinese and Vietnamese forces in waters claimed by both countries. Beijing's uncompromising approach to its South China Sea claims undermines its rhetoric of mutual respect and cooperation and raise real questions about what an Asia "run by Asians" will entail. Stripped of the rhetoric, Beijing's approach to Southeast Asia rests on three propositions: China's economic and military ascendancy is inevitable; for those that cooperate, the benefits will be extensive; for those that resist, the costs will be severe.

Beijing's campaign to exclude what it sees as non-regional powers from the region is similarly unrelenting. Chinese government officials rarely miss the opportunity when speaking at regional conferences to denounce all partnerships with Western countries as destabilising and resulting from outdated Cold War thinking. Naval and air patrols by the United States and its allies have been harassed by Chinese forces, which use non-lethal but extremely dangerous tactics to raise the risks to the patrolling craft. Australian ships and aircraft have been subjected to laser targeting, flares, sonar blasts and near collisions. The potential for escalation, particularly from clashes between Chinese and American patrols, is very real. It has become a contest of wills. Once again, the motivation and advantage lie very strongly in Beijing's favour.

*

Beijing's prospects for establishing a Sphere of Deference in Southeast Asia depend on its ability to convince the region of the inevitability, legitimacy and benefit of Chinese primacy. Given the ASEAN states' history of aversion to great-power domination, this will be no easy task. But here China has a valuable new asset: Southeast Asian governments are as disoriented as any by the Trump revolution. American tariffs designed to penalise the region's exporters for using Chinese components could be crippling to several economies and have prompted some to negotiate with Washington. A much more transactional and coercive United States opens up substantial opportunities for China to offer an alternative, more stable economic and security bloc – especially if Trump's successors confirm his preference for the management of global affairs by great powers in their own spheres of interest.

Australia needs to think clearly and carefully about what a Chinese-led Sphere of Deference to its north would look like. It would most likely be arranged on strongly hierarchic grounds, requiring Southeast Asian governments' deference to Beijing's preferences and requirements. It would also promote hierarchical politics within participating societies, seeking to guarantee their governing regimes against dissent or disruption. Beijing would seek to build its own legitimacy as regional leader, and foster solidarity among participating states, by promoting a strong anti-Western orientation and solidarity with the Global South. It would seek the extensive dependence of its southern neighbours on Chinese information technology and news content. It would propose a comprehensive mutual security guarantee, finding a grand bargain on the South China Sea in which Beijing retains its artificial island bases and nominal sovereignty, but engages with the other claimants on joint development and exploitation of resources. China would replace the United States as the guarantor of regional stability. It would seek to develop a common extended manufacturing, trade, investment and technology bloc with its southern hinterland, using the collective economic weight of the bloc to shape the global economy to its preferences.

This scenario would represent the most dangerous international situation Australia has ever faced. Unlike in 1942, when Australia faced possible incorporation into Japan's Greater East Asian Co-Prosperity Sphere, there would be little prospect of the United States, or any other great power for that matter, coming to our rescue. It would be a world in which, ultimately, Beijing determined Australia's use of Southeast Asia's skies and waterways, its access to markets, investment and imports, and its sources of diplomatic solidarity and support. Of course, all of these would ultimately depend on China's satisfaction with Australia's deference to its sensitivities and preferences. This would be a situation in which Australia would have to make constant choices between its sovereign values and its prosperity and international linkages. Unlike during World War II, a conventional conflict in which the US was already involved, this is a scenario that no external great power, however committed to supporting Australia, could help Canberra navigate. And especially not Trump's America.

THE AMERICAN WAY

The roots of American strategy in Asia predate the arrival of the First Fleet in Australia. In the immediate aftermath of the War of Independence, ships from New York, Boston and Baltimore began conducting a lucrative trade with imperial China. Their profits helped build the gleaming cities of the northeastern United States. As it looked to spread westwards, the new republic began to imagine a commercial empire in the Orient – a virtuous circle of trade and strength that would enable the thirteen states to overpower the British, French and Spanish interests that hemmed them in along the Atlantic coast.

So profitable was their engagement that the leaders of the new republic began to dream of global power. Alfred Thayer Mahan, a US Navy captain who had served in the Pacific, wrote compellingly of the mutual dynamic between maritime trade and naval (and thus global) power. President Theodore Roosevelt was an avid reader, as were the German kaiser and Japan's military leaders. Mahan also warned that the age of Asia's submission would be short-lived, and that the scale and vigour of its societies would soon make them major global actors. America was vulnerable to attack from across the Pacific, argued Mahan, and therefore would need to be attentive to the rise of great powers along Asia's Pacific coast.

For both access and protection, the United States became anxious to secure island bases across the Pacific, stepping stones for the projection of American power. The bloody conflict against Japan in World War II confirmed Mahan's warnings about America's vulnerability, and the Pacific theatre's battle of manoeuvre across the great archipelago showed both the advantages and vulnerabilities of island bases. At war's end, Washington was determined never to have to fight such a terrible campaign again. The new superpower required bases along the great archipelago that ran conveniently along the length of Asia's eastern coast. From ports and airstrips in Japan, Guam and the Philippines, as well as from aircraft carriers, the US could strike into the Asian mainland to contend with future challengers.

From the very start, American attention focused on China and Japan, as enrichment opportunities, possible allies and potential threats. Returning American missionaries built a fascination for both countries in middle America, giving domestic debates about them an enduring intensity. Having heavily backed the Nationalists in China's civil war, America was convulsed with alarm at the victory of Mao's communists. The first debate of the Cold War was over the question of "Who lost China?" The geopolitical imperative after the communist victory in China was to rehabilitate Japan's industrial economy and tie it to the West as a bulwark against revolutionary Marxism. Mao's victory generated an additional obligation for Washington: to defend the defeated Nationalist regime that had retreated to Taiwan. The North Korean attack on South Korea in 1950 saw the United States at war with a communist alliance of North Korea and China backed by the Soviet Union. That bitter conflict ended in stalemate and another obligation: to defend South Korea against renewed communist attack. All of these factors focused America's attention on Northeast Asia. Its alliances with Japan, South Korea, Taiwan and the Philippines, the location of its bases and aircraft carrier groups, were tightly calibrated to the containment of Chinese communism, preventing Soviet naval forays into the Pacific, and the defence of Japan, South Korea and Taiwan.

The intensity of this focus on Northeast Asia has left little if any interest and attention in Washington for Southeast Asia. Compared with the demographic, industrial and territorial behemoths in Northeast Asia, Southeast Asia has always seemed a strategic backwater to the American mind. Whenever it has featured, it has been as a consequence of American interest in something else. Its deepest involvement in the region, the agonising war fought in Vietnam between 1965 and 1975, was motivated by containing the spread of communism from China, rather than by any intrinsic concern with Southeast Asian geopolitics. Another fleeting era of US interest in Southeast Asia came early in the twenty-first century, when the region was designated as the second front in the War on Terror, after the 2002 Bali bombings. Once again it was a larger global goal that brought American attention, rather than an interest in the political stability of the region. Such has been the dearth of

American attention and knowledge that Washington has for long periods outsourced the monitoring of Southeast Asian affairs to its junior ally, Australia.

*

Australia's impulses to align its security interests and strategic thinking with America's predate Federation by decades. From the mid-nineteenth century the Australian colonies were looking to that "other branch of the Anglo-Saxon race," the United States, as a source of geopolitical inspiration. It was advocated that the Pacific become an "Anglo-Saxon Sea," and the language of "manifest destiny" was used to promote the annexation of islands in the Pacific. Opinion leaders soon began advocating for an Australian version of the Monroe Doctrine to warn hostile powers away from establishing bases in Australia's island approaches. When Prime Minister Alfred Deakin invited the American "Great White Fleet" to visit Australian ports in 1908, the visit was met with an outpouring of fraternal sentiment towards the US, with several newspapers arguing that America was a promising alternative ally to the waning might of Britain. By 1942, when American forces based themselves in Brisbane and began fighting alongside Australians to push back the Japanese, it seemed that the long-yearned-for Anglo-Saxon condominium in the Pacific had materialised.

The ANZUS Treaty of September 1951 was the price Washington paid to integrate Australia into its Cold War planning. Australia had raised concerns about American intentions to sign a non-punitive peace treaty with Japan and rehabilitate its economy. The US security guarantee was used to reassure Australia about the resurgence of Japanese militarism and aggression. In return, Canberra agreed to help contain communist expansion in the Middle East and Asia. It also toed Washington's line of diplomatically isolating Beijing. Soon Australian forces were fighting alongside Americans when the Korean War broke out in 1950, and then in the jungles of Vietnam from 1965. Through these operations and in allied consultations, strategic planners in Canberra gradually imbibed the geopolitical worldview that underpinned US Cold War strategy. Communism, ascendant in the Soviet Union and China, had seized the heart of the Eurasian continent, from which it was poised to bid for global supremacy. It was by nature expansionist, spreading across borders through subversion and by exploiting public discontent. And its spread was likely to be sequential – memorably, like a chain of falling dominoes.

Canberra willingly accepted the strategic corollary to this: that it was best to prevent communist aggression by containing its spread as close to the communist heartland as possible. It adopted a strategy of forward defence, sending Australian forces to fight alongside allies. Australia learnt the advantages and risks of subscribing to strategic goals that were far beyond its own capacity to achieve. Canberra could deal with threats a long way from its shores by leveraging the awesome power of its ally, but this required America to share Australia's threat perceptions. This was, and is, far from guaranteed. There was a mutual commitment dilemma at work: Australia risked being distracted from its immediate interests by the demands of its great-power ally, while the US was wary of being lured into a minor ally's local confrontations.

By the early 1960s, strategic planners had realised that they couldn't rely on the United States sharing Australia's interests in Southeast Asia. The left-leaning, assertive nationalism of Indonesian president Sukarno was viewed with greater anxiety in Canberra than in Washington. Whereas the US was inclined to accommodate Sukarno to ensure he didn't turn communist, Australia had major concerns about Indonesia's designs on West Irian and its confrontation with Malaya. An Australian "Strategic Position" statement in 1963 observed, "Australia could well be left to handle the situation [of conflict with Indonesia] without the assistance of the United States." These concerns intensified after the United States withdrew from Vietnam. From this realisation, a new defence framework developed, focusing on greater self-reliance. Launched by the Hawke government in 1987, the "Defence of Australia" strategy also necessitated a new diplomacy that sought to engage more deeply with Southeast Asia. Australia would, in a memorable phrase attributed to Paul Keating, "seek its security in Asia, rather than from Asia."

This led to a period of intensive diplomatic engagement, driven by an increasingly optimistic belief in Australia that economic integration with the booming economies of Asia would mean greater collective security. A focus on mutual enrichment would motivate all involved to sublimate their aggressive impulses. Regional institutions – ASEAN, APEC, the ASEAN Regional Forum and the East Asia Summit – would spread understandings of acceptable behaviour and common aspirations. Canberra's zeal came to worry its ally, as privately and publicly American policy-makers voiced concerns that the regionalist enthusiasm of Australia and its Asian neighbours was threatening to overshadow what the US saw as the real architecture: the system of American alliances stretching across the Pacific. On occasion Washington suspected Canberra of quietly seeking to exclude the United States from key forums such as APEC. The challenge of reconciling Australia's US alliance with its regional diplomacy became acute at times when American actions antagonised societies in Southeast Asia. Yet policy-makers in Canberra told themselves that there was no dilemma here: Australia's alliance with the United States was valued because it anchored a reassuring American presence in Southeast Asia. But over time there has been less and less reason to take comfort from this view.

*

For decades, many Southeast Asian governments regarded the combination of American regional predominance and inattention as a good thing. They could benefit from the stability provided by unchallenged American power without having to worry about the intrusions of an overbearing superpower. The experience of American covert intervention in Indonesian rebellions in the 1950s, and the full force of American combat power in the Vietnam War, showed how dangerous too much US attention could be. Alliances with the Philippines, Thailand and Australia, and access to bases in Singapore, kept the United States anchored in the region, reassuring even the most non-aligned of Southeast Asia's states that American inattention would not turn into a vacuum that would attract other powers into the region's affairs.

But the past half-century has seen the steady estrangement of Southeast Asia and America. In July 1969, during a stopover on Guam, President Richard

Nixon announced that America's willingness to defend Asian states had strict limits, and that they must look to their own resources to protect themselves. Three years later came a second Nixon shock, when the formerly hardline anti-communist president announced a rapprochement with communist China. Asia's non-communist states were caught by surprise, with no American consultation or forewarning to countries that had followed Washington in its diplomatic isolation of Mao's regime. Later that decade, there was no significant US response as communists took power in South Vietnam, Laos and Cambodia in 1975, or when Vietnam invaded Cambodia three years later.

American alliances in the region began unravelling. In 1977, the Southeast Asian Treaty Organisation (SEATO) was disestablished due to a lack of relevance and interest. With the atrophying of US alliances with Thailand and the Philippines in the 1990s, American forces lost access to basing facilities in Southeast Asia (the Philippines has since revived these). As the 1997 Asian financial crisis crippled Indonesia, Malaysia, Thailand and the Philippines, these societies reacted with bewilderment and then anger at Washington's detached and technocratic response to what regional governments saw as an existential emergency. Washington's occasional promotion of human rights and democracy in the region angered some of Southeast Asia's soft-authoritarian regimes, bringing together such erstwhile rivals as the Singaporean and Malaysian prime ministers to advocate "Asian values" as an alternative to Western liberal norms. The US-led invasion of Iraq (and, more recently, its support for Israel in the Gaza War) alienated many in the region, raising questions about the legitimacy of US power. By the time President Barack Obama declared that the United States would "pivot" towards the Pacific, the commitment was met with heavy scepticism in the region's policy circles. The surveys conducted by the Yusof Ishak Institute show that to Southeast Asian eyes American power and credibility are in continuous decline, both in absolute terms and in comparison with China's growing influence.

Southeast Asian doubts about America's commitment present Beijing with an opportunity. China's island-building in the South China Sea is a direct challenge to the credibility of the United States as the paramount power in the Pacific. Beijing is aggressive towards the Philippines in the waters where both countries have competing claims precisely because it is a treaty ally of the US. China realises that the rest of the region is watching closely the extent to which Washington is willing to support its closest Southeast Asian ally in standing up to its much larger neighbour. The record so far is not flattering to the United States. At no point has the US intervened or threatened to intervene in a confrontation with Chinese forces on behalf of its treaty ally, relying instead on bolstering the Philippines' own capabilities. These "grey zone" tactics – aggressive, but beneath the military threshold – are low-risk, high-reward for China: it can control the pace and scale of confrontation with a smaller, weaker opponent. For the United States to intervene on behalf of its smaller ally, by contrast, risks bringing on an escalating crisis with a highly capable opponent.

Washington's reaction to a direct challenge from China has been instructive. There has been no sustained effort to restore America's credibility or perceptions of its commitment to Southeast Asia. There have been surges of attention and largesse followed by troughs of lassitude, when Washington's focus has been drawn elsewhere. The regular non-appearance of American presidents at the annual East Asia Summit, the main forum through which ASEAN engages with its partners, speaks volumes about US attention and priorities.

*

As the Cold War came to an end, policy-makers in Canberra and Tokyo worried that the United States would withdraw from Asia. They were relieved when Washington recast the rationale of its alliances from defending against communist expansion to promoting a stable, globalising world order. America and its allies would replace containment with enlargement of the community of liberal democracies committed to the rule of law and free trade. The biggest prize would be China: even if it didn't become a liberal democracy as had Japan, South Korea and Taiwan, perhaps it would become a stable, rule-abiding soft-authoritarian state like Singapore.

Since normalising relations with Beijing, Washington had come to view China's growing involvement in regional and global affairs according to its own, liberal form of economic determinism. A bipartisan consensus believed that China's growing prosperity and connectedness with the world beyond its borders would have liberalising social and political impacts. Enthusiastic American economic, political and academic embrace of China would unleash irresistible forces of moderation and collaboration in a country that had once seen itself as in the vanguard of world revolution. Most importantly, a liberalising China would not challenge the global status quo, or America's leading role in it. In New York in September 2005, George W. Bush's deputy secretary of state, Robert Zoellick, called on China to become a "responsible stakeholder," shouldering "a responsibility to strengthen the international system that has enabled its success."

It was the last gasp of hopeful optimism about China's prospects for socialisation into the status quo. Soon after, the 2008 global financial crisis hollowed out America's and Europe's legitimacy as leaders of the global economy. Beijing's confidence and assertiveness intensified after Xi Jinping's elevation to Chinese president, which dispelled any illusions that China was liberalising or democratising. Xi's anti-corruption campaign showcased a harder, more capable and ruthless authoritarianism. It became clearer that Beijing saw the United States not as a partner but as a rival.

Almost overnight, bipartisan optimism about China turned into bipartisan alarm. With the chastened zeal of the recently disabused, America's strategic analysts began to produce an avalanche of reports on the scale, nature and danger of China's frontal assault on America's role in Asia and the world. Many pointed out Beijing's development of missiles, submarines and drones that would put US naval assets and bases in the western Pacific at high risk in the event of hostilities. The scale of China's military build-up began to cause alarm, particularly when it became clear that it had surpassed America's naval assets and was extending its lead. China's diplomatic gambits, such as the BRI, the AIIB and BRICS (a grouping originally comprising Brazil, Russia, India and China), were interpreted as ways to leverage the scale and dynamism of the Chinese economy for strategic benefit. New forms of coercion, such as provocative air and naval patrols, were taken as evidence that China was another of the expansionist authoritarian powers that the US had serially faced down over the past century.

American strategists recognise that the contest with China in Asia is a home game for Beijing and an away game for Washington. The United States has therefore become more reliant on its partners in Asia and the Pacific. During the Cold War, Japan, South Korea, the Philippines, Thailand and Australia were largely passive recipients of US security guarantees and providers of bases and intelligence facilities. Now US allies, and particularly Japan and Australia, are needed as active contributors and partners. India is courted through the Quad as a potential Asian counterbalance against Chinese power. These conversations, between the United States and its treaty allies, and between its allies and other states in the region, are based on the premise that what threatens the US threatens the region, and that any strategy that seeks to maintain American predominance is for the good of all.

*

As the United States refocused on countering the challenge from a rising China, it dragged Australia's strategic attention with it. There was a period of cognitive dissonance in Canberra, in which the importance of strategic alignment with the US grated against the super-cycle of wealth creation that Australia's trade with China was generating. These years, from 2008 to 2016, revealed clearly just how different Australian and American incentives were when it came to China. Australia's economy was highly complementary with China's, supercharging development and creating wealth on both sides. By contrast, China's manufacturing juggernaut appeared to be hollowing out the US manufacturing base. Viewing China as a predatory competitor which was stealing intellectual property and subsidising excess manufacturing capacity, Washington took the easy step of designating it as a strategic competitor. In Canberra, where evidence of an ongoing China boom was everywhere to see, that was not so easy. Despite growing concerns about

China's behaviour in the South China Sea and signs of its activism in domestic politics, Australian governments continued building positive relations. Even as the United States began ramping up its language and thinking of China as a strategic competitor, Australia announced a comprehensive strategic partnership and a free trade agreement with China. Ignoring Washington's warnings, it became a member of China's AIIB.

This was the most serious divergence of Australian and American interests since the era of Australia's regional institution-building at the end of the Cold War. American policy-makers were clearly worried that China's sheer economic gravity would drag Australia away from the alliance. They shouldn't have been. The effects of initiatives put in place during that earlier era of divergence would soon deliver Canberra into much closer alignment with Washington. Four post–Cold War developments have combined to substantially increase the influence of American perceptions and preoccupations in Canberra.

The Australian American Leadership Dialogue was conceived during a 1992 yacht cruise on Sydney Harbour as part of the official visit by US president George H.W. Bush. With the passing of the "Coral Sea generation" of Australians who remembered America coming to Australia's rescue during World War II, it was thought a new initiative was needed to shore up solidarity. The annual Dialogue brings together Australian and American politicians, officials, businesspeople, academics and journalists. The discussions are both formal and informal, developing a familiarity and rapport between regular participants from each side. Those held in Washington, such as the one I attended in 2006, are lavished with imperial grandeur: a visit to the White House, a reception on the state department rooftop, an audience with the vice president. The Dialogue has proliferated into multiple engagements and initiatives, building a cadre of devotees to the alliance relationship, and deliberately drawing in the opinion leaders and rising stars of both countries.

Then there is "G'Day USA," a year-long program of events to promote Australia's art and culture to American audiences. Movie stars, musicians, celebrity chefs and billionaires "showcase Australia's creative, innovative economy and society" and affirm the centrality of the United States to Australia's wellbeing and success. Australia does nothing of comparable scale and regularity with any other country.

A third element of the Americanisation of Australia's strategic and intellectual culture is the proliferation of American-style, US-leaning think-tanks. For much of the twentieth century, Australia was largely a backwater in think-tank terms. But early in the new millennium, that began to change. The Lowy Institute was founded by a billionaire in Sydney; the Australian Strategic Policy Institute (ASPI) started with the support of the federal government in Canberra; the United States Studies Centre opened at the University of Sydney; and then the Perth USAsia Centre arrived in Western Australia. All were considerably better funded than existing Australian think-tanks, and all began producing reports designed to critique and influence Australian government policy. Their business models were lifted from their counterparts in Washington, DC, as were their high publication values and focus on media messaging. All are notably pro-American, and ASPI is extremely hawkish on China. All heavily influence the strategic ecosystem in Canberra, where officials cannot escape the influence of their reports and media commentary.

A fourth element is the progressive embedding of US experience into the career trajectories of Australia's defence, foreign policy and intelligence officials. The patterns of travel, postings and embedding take Australian officials repeatedly to the centres of American strategy in Asia: Washington, DC, and Honolulu. Their status as close allies ushers them into the inner sanctums of US policy-making and intelligence analysis, where they are simply expected to share the assumptions and perceptions of their hosts. This is a process of intensive and sustained socialisation into the thought patterns and values of our major ally that is very difficult for an ambitious Australian official to avoid. Career progression in Canberra starts to rely on the ability to reproduce what appear to be verities about Australo-American geopolitical imperatives in Asia.

Australia's period of cognitive dissonance came to an end relatively abruptly after 2015. Canberra's perceptions of China, and the strategy for facing down Beijing, aligned seamlessly with Washington's. Notably, it was

Malcolm Turnbull, who before becoming prime minister had called for Australia to adopt a balanced and nuanced policy towards China, who led the reorientation. Despite his intelligence and experience, Turnbull was no match for the powerful and consistent messages he was receiving from the strategic ecosystem in which he as prime minister was embedded.

*

However, the new Australian-American strategic solidarity is about to shift radically, leaving Australia stranded with an outdated conception of shared interests. When the second Trump administration published its National Security Strategy in November 2025, predictably it attracted immediate derision. But to dismiss this document would be to repeat the mistake of underestimating Trump and his impact on US and world events. What this short, 29-page document heralds is a radical shift in America's approach to geopolitics – a shift that has been foreshadowed in US actions in the world since the start of Trump's second term. The strategy simultaneously narrows and expands how America defines security, focusing hard on the need to "protect and defend our economy and our people from harm," while identifying a greater range of threats, including predatory trade practices, cultural subversion and mass migration, as the appropriate subjects of US defence planning. In true MAGA fashion, it commits US strategy to amassing ever greater power as an intrinsic objective, with little thought to the ends of that power. But most significant is its single-minded concern with economic competition. The underpinnings of US grand strategy have shifted from geopolitics to geoeconomics, as Washington uses the full force of its statecraft to shift international economic transactions in its favour, using economic coercion to achieve strategic goals. Alliances shift from security partnerships to economic networks, and allies are co-opted into helping deliver on American geoeconomic interests.

There are two implications of the National Security Strategy that should be ringing alarm bells in Canberra. The first is a dramatic shift in the US attitude towards states it has traditionally referred to as "peer competitors." Whereas China and Russia were once (including by the first Trump administration) seen as challengers to US primacy, to be either faced down or co-opted, this National Security Strategy seeks to develop stable terms of coexistence with Beijing and Moscow. It also discusses at length the need for the United States to focus on the Western Hemisphere, excluding other powers from its geopolitical backyard. In a nutshell, the strategy conjures a vision of great powers developing mutually exclusive spheres of interest to manage global affairs. This is a hierarchic model of international relations. It is fundamentally corrosive of the egalitarian model of world order based on the sovereign equality of states, which has been enshrined in international law and order institutions such as the United Nations for the last eighty years.

The second worrying implication for Canberra is what the National Security Strategy (and, indeed, Trump's actions to date) signals about American interests in Asia. For the first time in over two centuries, a US administration has ceased to see Asia as an economic opportunity and started to speak and act in ways that cast the region as an economic menace. China and its manufacturing networks throughout Asia are seen as manifest threats to American prosperity and jobs. Trump's tariffs are a way of decoupling the United States from these trade and investment links, which are hollowing out the US economy, and forcing Asian countries to accept trading relations on American terms. The strategy is evasive about what previous administrations have worried about – the rise of a "peer competitor" in Asia – instead prioritising mutual restraint and stable great-power relations. Allies and partners will now assist the US "to counteract predatory economic practices and use our combined economic power to help safeguard our prime position in the global economy." As Asia is recast from economic opportunity to economic threat and hit with punitive tariffs to force negotiated agreements with Washington, US engagement looks less like reassurance and more like extortion.

There are few overt signs that policy-makers in Canberra have registered this profound shift in how our major ally sees our region, and how this affects Australia's policy choices.

For over a century, Australia has pondered how it should relate to the societies to its north. It is a never-resolved debate, evolving with the circumstances, recurring with each generation. One impulse has been to think about how different they are from Australian society and how corrupting intimate contact might be, and to resolve to keep them as far at bay as possible. But there's been another reaction as well, one that thinks about our commonalities with societies in Asia. There's geographic proximity, of course. But there's also from time to time developed a sense of shared destinies – either a sense of a common threat such as war and invasion, as in World War II, or a sense of a common interest in stability, development and peace.

The discourse of difference was the dominant narrative in Australian society for the first half-century after Federation. But after about 1955, Australian awareness of shared interests with our northern neighbours started to become ascendant. The policy artifacts of the discourse of difference became increasingly uncomfortable. Primary among these was the White Australia policy, which a growing number of Australians began to see would be an impediment to developing close relations with the newly independent states of Asia. Initially, education scholarships were used to try to compensate for the offence caused by the racially restrictive immigration policy; eventually the policy was progressively abandoned, then dismantled.

By that time, it had become much clearer that Australia shared many of the aspirations of its northern neighbours. They were pragmatic and focused on their own economic development. Even if non-aligned, they were generally inclined towards the West and against communism. They were strong supporters of the sovereign equality of states. They were committed multilateralists, having founded ASEAN and fully engaged with the United Nations, the World Bank and with globalism generally. As their economies boomed serially – starting with Japan's remarkable postwar recovery, and followed by South Korea, Taiwan, Hong Kong, Singapore and then other Southeast Asian economies – Australia became increasingly tied to their success. Demand for Australian products – agriculture, minerals, energy – increased as Asian economies grew, more than compensating for the United Kingdom's entry into the European Economic Community.

Acceptance of pragmatic commonality began to turn to admiration as the Australian economy faltered and sputtered through the late 1970s while the Asian economies boomed. The success of its northern neighbours became an admonition to Australia, that it needed to change to become more dynamic. As the 1980s progressed, they started to be thought of as more than neighbours: they were Australia's region. Australia's fate was seen as increasingly tied to the countries to its north – not only our economy but also our security. The knowledge gulf of Australian society about its northern neighbours came to be seen as a problem, while engagement with its region came to be viewed as an essential part of the evolution of modern Australia.

Almost miraculously, Asia's biggest and most fearsome state started to follow the same pragmatic, developmentalist pathway by the 1980s. China, once the exporter of revolution and subversion, and Asia's most trenchant opponent of the West, quietly ended support for communist insurgents in Southeast Asia and embarked on a process of normalisation of relations with the West and the region. For Australian governments, Coalition and Labor, China came to be seen as an integral part of the Asia boom story: culturally and politically different but committed to the same path as the other surging economies around it. Prime ministers Hawke, Keating and Howard believed Australia had a special role in ushering China into the region and the world. Australia became an evangelist for China's acceptance, offering vociferous support for its inclusion in the institutions of belonging: APEC, the ASEAN Regional Forum, the World Trade Organization.

As Australia embarked on its own journey of economic renewal – floating the dollar, deregulating the financial sector, lowering trade barriers – its leaders became true believers in the transformative power of openness and economic development. Development was the ultimate solvent for hidebound ideological commitments and sclerotic policy settings; it was the ultimate source of regime legitimacy. As people became wealthier and more secure, they would expect governments to behave in ways that would deliver more of the same. Whenever Australian prime ministers visited China, they saw this logic at work. In the proliferating bridges and roads, the gleaming serried high-rise towers, the space-age airport terminals, they saw more than economic development; they imagined social and political transformation also.

Australia came to imagine itself as part of a region of states that had sublimated every disruptive impulse to the goals of stability and economic success. In enriching themselves, they enriched Australia also. None more so than China, which developed a voracious appetite for Australian minerals, energy, agricultural produce and education. In the series of cautious leaders they encountered, from Deng Xiaoping through Jiang Zemin to Hu Jintao, Australian prime ministers from Malcolm Fraser to John Howard found pragmatic developmentalists who would allow China to evolve, if not into a fully fledged democracy as in South Korea and Taiwan, then perhaps towards the sort of soft authoritarianism they found in Singapore or Suharto's Indonesia. Bob Hawke's tears after the Tiananmen Square massacre in 1989 were those of shocked disillusionment; disbelief that a regime in which he had invested so much hope for liberalisation had acted so brutally. But the Tiananmen shock wore off quickly in Canberra, and soon all of Australia's optimistic engagement with China had resumed.

Even as its great-power ally began to cool on China, Australia kept faith. Beginning with the Reagan administration, US governments started to raise concerns about China's human rights record and unfair trade practices. The Tiananmen massacre saw both the United States and Australia suspend cooperation with Beijing, but Australia became the Western state that acted earliest to re-normalise relations. Howard claimed to have developed a distinctively Australian way of dealing with China that could serve as an example to others:

> The relationship between Australia and China is sound because it is built upon the important principles of mutual respect for each other and a recognition that different societies that have different cultures

> and different histories can nevertheless work together very closely if they understand those differences and they focus on the things that can bring their two societies together.

During Howard's tenure, the things that brought the two societies together seemed to overwhelm the differences. China's surging demand for our exports carried us unscathed through the Asian financial crisis, the dotcom slump and the global financial crisis, to rack up a three-decade run of uninterrupted prosperity. Howard's successor, Kevin Rudd, took the enthusiasm even further. Believing in the power of the mutuality of Sino–Australian interests, Rudd tried to convince Beijing to treat Australia as a *zhengyou* – a friend uniquely allowed to criticise China's human rights practices in public, in China itself. Beijing's furious reaction marked the beginning of the end of Australia's Sino-optimism.

*

The Beijing Olympics in 2008 were dubbed China's coming-out party: a chance to showcase the new China to the world: fast-developing, confident and reassuringly focused on sporting success. But the games took place against a background of worrying developments. The global financial crisis that crippled the American and European economies foregrounded for the first time China's inexorable economic growth. It was predicted that the once-cloistered economy would surpass America's in size in a matter of decades. That same year China's claims to the South China Sea became more assertive, its clashes with competing claimants more regular and unyielding. In Australia, the Olympic torch procession was marred by ugly clashes between demonstrators protesting China's human rights policies and pro-Beijing groups who appeared to have been encouraged and assisted by the Chinese embassy in Canberra. In 2009, a government in Canberra led by a Mandarin-speaking prime minister issued a defence white paper that spoke forebodingly of China's military build-up. Diplomatic cables published by Wikileaks reported Prime Minister Rudd warning American Secretary of State Hillary Clinton that Washington should be prepared to use force against a resurgent China.

In 2012 a very different leader rose to the Chinese presidency. Xi Jinping, the son of a revolutionary hero, criticised his predecessors Deng, Jiang and Hu for allowing too much liberalisation of the Chinese economy, and for being too obsequious to the West. Rather than being partners in China's development, Xi cast Western countries as a threat, saying in a 2013 speech: "Western countries see our country's development and expansion as a challenge to their values, systems and models" and consequently they were mounting a campaign of "ideological and cultural infiltration of our country." Taking the collapse of the Soviet Union as a warning, Xi moved to intensify China's commitment to Marxist ideology, to rein in capitalist excess, and to increase public surveillance and the operation of a social credit system in Chinese society. Under Xi, China would become much more forthright in asserting its interests.

Policy-makers in Canberra were thrown off balance by this new China with much sharper edges. China's demand for Australia's exports continued to deliver the largest surge in national wealth since the 1950s. On the other hand, Beijing's militarised island-building in the South China Sea constituted the most significant shift in Australia's strategic context since the end of World War II. Mainland Australia was now within direct striking distance of Chinese bombers, effectively eliminating the strategic space on which Australian defence planning had been based. At least in public, mounting alarm crowded out careful analysis. Lurid hyperbole began bubbling to the surface. Australia's intelligence agencies began to warn of Chinese subversion that would deliver a compliant Australia without the need for any coercive action by Beijing. A former director-general of ASIO warned that Australians could soon "wake up to find decisions made in our country that are not in the interests of the country," with a foreign power "pulling the strings from offshore."

On leaving office, Howard reflected with pride on his government's ability to strengthen Australia's relationships with China and the United States at the same time. But as American apprehensions grew about China, senior officials in Washington began to articulate their worries about how close Canberra was getting to Beijing. As early as 1999, senior Republican Rich

Armitage warned that the alliance would not survive if Australia refused to support the United States in a conflict over Taiwan. The real US worry was about Australia's growing economic dependence. Addressing a joint sitting of parliament in Canberra in 2014, President Barack Obama warned that "economic partnerships can't just be about one nation extracting another's resources." By 2019 the newly arrived US ambassador, Arthur Culvahouse, told a Canberra audience that as he was leaving Washington he had been asked by concerned members of Congress, "Who lost Australia?" to China. These were public statements from both sides of American politics; there is no doubt that versions of the same message were communicated in hundreds of private meetings between American and Australian officials. The core point was that Australia was playing a dangerous game in becoming so economically dependent on China; security and prosperity were not complementary – they were alternatives. American officials became increasingly irritated by the formula – first articulated by Howard – that Australia "didn't have to choose" between the US and China; increasingly, they were adamant that, actually, Australia did have to choose.

Australia's booming trade and investment relationship with China started to be characterised not as an opportunity but as a risk. Former prime minister Tony Abbott told an audience in Japan that Australia's over-reliance on China was its "deepest complacency, trading off long-term national security for short-term economic gain." The accusation, according to historian James Curran, was that "Australia had been betrayed by its political and intellectual elites, who had been duped and duchessed by China." The growing orthodoxy was that Australia was in danger of being reeled in by the same deal that the CCP had perpetrated on the Chinese people: access to ever-greater wealth in return for obedience to Beijing's will. Such claims became startlingly real when it was revealed in 2017 that Labor senator Sam Dastyari, who had been publicly supportive of Beijing's claims in the South China Sea, had benefited from the largesse of two Beijing-aligned businessmen. Gradually, a willingness to trade with China, to accept Chinese investment or students, began to be portrayed as disloyalty: a betrayal of Australia, and a betrayal of our US allies. Institutions that advocated a more nuanced, less alarmist view of China, such as the Australia-China Relations Institute at the University of Technology, Sydney, were subjected to intense scrutiny over their financing. China Matters, a bipartisan initiative dedicated to bringing together the separate discussions of Australia's economic and security interests with China, was defunded by the Morrison government, which then actively blocked its application for deductable gift recipient status – in effect shutting it down. Any deviation from the orthodoxy was to be targeted and suppressed. In this Manichean view of the world, the ultimate test of Australia's alliance loyalty would be to suffer the economic consequences that would flow from Beijing's displeasure.

Further deadening the Australian government's capacity for careful reassessment of its interests in the face of a more assertive China was the increasingly partisan politics swirling around foreign policy. Since 1996, questioning opponents' foreign policy credentials has become an increasingly common aspect of election campaigns. Then, it was Prime Minister Paul Keating questioning the Coalition's acceptability in Asia; by 2007 it was the Howard government proposing that Opposition leader Kevin Rudd would be a "Manchurian candidate," far too sympathetic to Beijing to protect Australia's interests. In 2021, Prime Minister Scott Morrison accused Opposition leader Anthony Albanese of "backing in the Chinese government," while his defence minister, Peter Dutton, accused the Labor Party of being weak on national security. The old trope of appeasement of Hitler at Munich was wielded against anyone who dared to disagree with what was rapidly becoming the dominant security narrative. By 2016, the China threat narrative had also become bipartisan. A group of parliamentarians from the Coalition and Labor began to refer to themselves as the Wolverines, after a group of students from a 1980s B-movie who resist a communist invasion of America. They went so far as to paste stickers on their Parliament House office doors depicting claw scratches, but their advocacy of a hard line on China gave their party leaders little room for nuance or genuine questioning of policy.

*

Labor and then Coalition governments began to take tentative steps to ensure Australia was not drawn too closely into China's economic orbit. In 2010, the Gillard government blocked the Chinese telecommunications giant Huawei from bidding to build the National Broadband Network. The Foreign Investment Review Board became much more active in screening and blocking Chinese investment bids. But at least initially, such moves were balanced by positive engagement. In 2014, the two countries agreed to designate their relationship a "comprehensive strategic partnership" and in 2015 inaugurated a China–Australia Free Trade Agreement. But after 2016, Australia's statements and actions became steadily more confrontational. Canberra publicly backed the ruling of the Permanent Court of Arbitration against China's claims in the South China Sea and joined the United States in conducting freedom-of-navigation operations there and through the Taiwan Strait. As if to show that a balancing coalition against China was in the making, Canberra took part enthusiastically in the revival of the Quadrilateral Strategic Dialogue with the United States, India and Japan – all countries with rivalrous relations with Beijing.

Shocked by ASIO revelations of two large-scale Chinese hacks of computers in Parliament House, and several other attempts to gain influence, Prime Minister Malcolm Turnbull introduced foreign interference legislation to parliament in late 2017. Turnbull intoned: "Modern China was founded by the statement that Chinese people have stood up. And today, and every day, the Australian people stand up and assert their sovereignty in our nation, with our parliament and our law." It seemed to be, and was interpreted in Beijing as, a deliberate insult, by comparing Australia's resistance to Chinese interference with China's own resistance against imperialism. The following year the government blocked Chinese telecommunications companies Huawei and ZTE from bidding to help develop Australia's 5G network. And then in April 2020, Foreign Minister Marise Payne used an appearance on Sunday morning political analysis program *Insiders* to call for an independent international inquiry into the origins of the Covid-19 pandemic. Prime Minister Scott Morrison backed the call a few days later, suggesting the international inspectors should have powers akin to those of UN weapons inspectors. Beijing responded with increasingly angry statements, and in May 2020 began restricting an expanding range of Australian exports. Official relations were placed in the deep freeze.

While measures taken to increase Australia's resilience were justified, no strategy or rationale was ever publicly articulated for the increasing stridency of Australia's actions and words. This is not surprising, given that there is no evidence of a careful, systematic appraisal of how Australia's interests were affected by a more assertive China. But there is plenty of evidence from which we can infer the Australian government's motives. An initial and enduring impulse seems to have been to demonstrate Australian courage, the willingness of a smaller country to stand up to a larger bully. This played into a range of public myths and tropes, from the Anzac legend of battling against overwhelming odds to the regular self-congratulation we offer ourselves for "punching above our weight" on the global stage. Another calculation seems to have been that by "calling China out" for bad behaviour, Australia would effectively embarrass Beijing into moderating its claims and actions. James Curran reports on a 2017 briefing in Sydney by a senior DFAT official which included this claim: "We need to call them on it – that we know what they are up to. This will make China see the costs of its behaviour. And by doing this Canberra can exploit Beijing's sensitivity to being ganged up on by the region." This was of a piece with Australia's frequent calls for the defence of the international "rules-based order" – a not-so-oblique reference to China's activities and claims in the South China Sea and East China Sea.

Another impulse was to demonstrate to other countries, particularly in Southeast Asia and the Pacific, that coercive capabilities and intent lay behind Beijing's blandishments of win-win cooperation. By provoking Beijing's "wolf warrior" diplomacy and economic coercion, Canberra was claiming a leadership role in helping other countries understand the true nature of the China threat. Turnbull alluded to this strategy in his 2017 speech at Singapore's Shangri-La Dialogue, warning that:

> A coercive China would find its neighbours resenting demands they cede their autonomy and strategic space, and look[ing] to counterweight Beijing's power by bolstering alliances and partnerships, between themselves and especially with the United States.

By revealing China's coercive capabilities, Australia could kick-start a balancing response by the region.

A further motive was to reassure the United States that Australia was not being captured by China as American officials feared; rather, Australia was prepared to court possible economic retaliation by playing a leading role in pushing back against Beijing. Once the decision had been taken by the National Security Committee of cabinet to ban Huawei and ZTE, Prime Minister Turnbull called US President Donald Trump to inform him of the decision, which he claimed to be the first formal ban on the Chinese telcos anywhere in the world. This drew on an old playbook: seeking an even closer relationship with Washington through an ostentatious act of loyalty at significant cost. The price of maintaining the alliance would be Australia's relationship with China.

*

In the space of not much more than five years, the foundations of Australia's relations with Asia were recast. Rather than regarding the region as a source of opportunity, with which it shared common, and indeed complementary, interests, Australia had come to see it as a source of incessant threat. So large did the perception of China's malevolence loom in the national official imagination that it had come to colour every other calculation in Australian foreign policy. Relations with other countries in Asia began to be evaluated and managed according to how closely that country shared Australia's perceptions of China. India and Japan, each with longstanding territorial disputes with China and deeply held strategic distrust of Beijing, were lifted to the front rank of Australia's foreign policy priorities. So, too, the Philippines and Vietnam, which had been the most forthright in defending their territorial claims in the South China Sea. With other states in Southeast Asia, Australian foreign policy seemed rudderless, frenetic in developing bilateral initiatives but lacking the sense of overall direction and conviction they once had. For example, Canberra's defence agreements, dialogues and joint exercises with Southeast Asian countries have increased by 25 per cent since 2017, but these have not brought our northern neighbours' positions on China any closer to Australia's. Similarly, Australia lost its once-evangelical belief in the region's multilateral institutions, even those, such as APEC and the ASEAN Regional Forum, that it had helped to found. It has been many years since Canberra has advocated for a major initiative through a regional institution, and the post-summit statements issued year after year show a collective loss of ambition.

The China threat has become the cracked lens through which Australia looks at the world. Anywhere that China seems to be succeeding in developing influence is taken as a zero-sum loss for Canberra. The ability to counter Beijing's moves in Southeast Asia and the Pacific has come to be seen as a vital indicator of government competence. The announcement of a security agreement between China and Solomon Islands during the 2022 federal election campaign was seized on by the Labor Opposition and dubbed "the worst strategic failure" since 1942 – when Japan seized Solomon Islands. While the Albanese government successfully reset relations with Beijing after its victory in the May 2022 election, restoring a sense of normalcy to bilateral ties, the underlying fearful stance towards China remains unchanged. Foreign Minister Penny Wong's pragmatic statements don't mask an underlying conviction that Canberra's and Beijing's interests and intentions are irreconcilable. At the 2024 Australia–China Strategic Economic Dialogue – restarted under the Albanese government – she said, "dialogue enables us to manage our differences; we both know we will not eliminate them. Australia will always be Australia and China will always be China."

*

The aims that drove Australia's shift to confront China have not been achieved, and this should have provoked serious rethinking in Canberra.

If standing up to China was meant to demonstrate Australia's courage, the opposite has occurred: Australia has become ever more fearful and dependent on the United States over the last decade. "Calling out" Beijing's behaviour so as to curb its aggression has seen some success: after 2021 there is clear evidence that China's "wolf warrior" abrasiveness and economic coercion have been wound back. It would be a mistake, however, to attribute this wholly to plucky little Australia. China-watcher Richard McGregor demonstrates that it is a broader international coalition of criticism and concern about China's behaviour that has motivated Beijing's more moderate stance. Australia appears to have reassured Washington that it is in no danger of being "lost" to China, and Morrison's AUKUS deal may have been partly a quid-pro-quo for Australia's self-harming stand. But despite its reassurances that the United States "would not leave Australia alone on the field," there is little evidence of Washington directly intervening to support Australia while it faced Beijing's economic coercion. Indeed, it has become clear that American exporters were direct beneficiaries, moving in to supply products to China that were no longer accepted from Australia. And there is scant evidence that Malcolm Turnbull's hope – that demonstrating Beijing's coercive tendencies would trigger a balancing coalition against China – has been realised. To the contrary, Canberra's efforts to mobilise a balancing reaction to China have had the effect of eroding Australia's standing with its northern neighbours – the ultimate act of strategic self-harm.

Ten years on, Australia's China-threat foreign policy is now bipartisan. The Albanese government has toned down the confrontational rhetoric and resumed high-level meetings with China, but it has not reduced the level of alarm about China's challenge to Australia's interests and way of life. This shows how completely entrenched the single-minded focus on the China challenge has become in our institutions of government, our media and our public discussions. As a result, we have adopted American strategic planning as our own approach, and become more deeply embedded in the US response to China than ever before.

What we have not had is a clear and balanced discussion of the menace China poses to Australia. There is much talk of threats, but little of consequences – how serious they might be and how to rank them. So let's try to lay this out.

In our national conversation, there are four basic ways in which China is seen to threaten Australia and its interests. Beijing is most often publicly accused of trying to subvert our values and undermine our institutions. But for all the regular intelligence announcements about the scale of Chinese espionage in this country, there is scant evidence that vital Australian institutions have actually been compromised. If Beijing has been committed to the systematic subversion or undermining of our basic institutions and values, it appears to have been particularly unsuccessful thus far. Senator Sam Dastyari stands alone as the sole case of successful buying of influence that has come to light, and it is likely he stands as a salutary example to other parliamentarians. Moreover, what is seldom acknowledged is the resilience of Australian institutions, the increasing vigilance of society to cyber threats, intellectual property theft and overt propaganda, and the robust integrity of our electoral systems, our judicial processes and our financial regulation.

Another regularly discussed threat is Beijing's use of our close trading relationship to coerce and intimidate Australia, but once more the evidence for its effectiveness is scant. Between 2020 and 2023, Beijing imposed what

Richard McGregor has called "the most comprehensive punitive trade measures it has used against any country in recent history" against Australian coal, barley, meat, wine, lobsters and timber. In November 2020 the Chinese embassy in Canberra handed a journalist a list of fourteen demands Australia would need to meet before Beijing would consider ending its economic coercion. These included dropping the ban on Huawei bidding for the 5G network; revising Australia's foreign interference laws; dropping its calls for an international inquiry into the origins of Covid-19; refraining from criticising China's human rights record in Tibet and Xinjiang; and preventing criticism of China by media outlets and think-tanks. The Australian government yielded to none of these demands; indeed, it is hard to imagine an Australian government of either side of politics surviving were it to accede to such blatantly coercive demands against core liberal-democratic values. In the end, the Productivity Commission concluded the trade restrictions cost less than 1 per cent of GDP during the almost three years they were in operation. It appears that despite Australia's strong trade links with China, Beijing has little actual coercive leverage against Canberra. It is also seldom discussed what leverage Australia would have over China were it prepared to wield its own instruments of economic coercion.

Third, there have been regular references to China's military build-up and its consequent ability to threaten Australia with direct military attack. Certainly, China has the capability to mount physical attacks against Australia and its interests. The airstrips, missile batteries and docking facilities it has constructed in the South China Sea have put Beijing's offensive military options thousands of kilometres closer to Australia. The Chinese naval task group that circumnavigated Australia in early 2025 was an impressive display of the reach of China's maritime force and the range of attack options that would be open to it. According to one analyst, "It's almost as though the force was tailored to emphasise just how insignificant Australia's dwindling military is against its northern neighbour." The real question, however, is under what circumstances China would want to attack Australia. The only conceivable circumstance under which a military attack would occur is in the event of a major war between China and the United States. This would see the US using intelligence sourced from the joint intelligence facility at Pine Gap, and probably Tindall air base and HMAS *Stirling* naval base in its combat operations. It is likely, therefore, that China would seek to eliminate these capabilities by direct military attack. It is hard to think of another scenario in which the stakes would be high enough for China to physically attack Australia.

Finally, Beijing could threaten our national interests by shaping the regional order in Southeast Asia to increasingly exclude Australia. As we've seen, China's objective is to develop a Sphere of Deference so that Southeast Asia's states comply with China's wishes when it comes to its interests and the legitimacy of the CCP. Beijing's rhetoric casts the United States and other Western states as inimical to Asian states managing their own affairs. It seeks to bind Southeast Asia's economies ever more tightly to China's own economy, through infrastructure, technology and integrating them into its global manufacturing chains. The danger of Beijing shifting the regional status quo towards hostility to Australia's interests is arguably the most overlooked aspect of the China challenge in Australian official thinking. This could potentially imperil our prosperity, our trade and air routes, and crucial diplomatic partnerships and memberships. It would leave Australia dangerously isolated diplomatically and strategically, unable to influence regional institutions and commitments that would affect our vital interests. And it is an objective on which Beijing has set a priority, shaping what it sees as its hinterland as the platform for its rise to global power.

*

The essence of strategy is assessing how a particular development affects national interests, and what priority we should give it. It looks at likelihoods and consequences. The four threats most often raised in the Australian conversation – subversion, coercion, direct attack and reshaping our region – have different likelihoods and consequences. Subversion is high likelihood, low consequence. The covert manipulation of information, opinion and media content is becoming easier to attempt, thanks to changes in information technologies, and therefore more prevalent. However, the record shows that Australia's society and institutions are resilient and growing more vigilant against subversion.

Economic coercion is also high likelihood, low consequence. It is a tactic used repeatedly by Beijing against other countries; quite possibly it will be directed once more at Australia. But again, Australia appears to be largely impervious to such a campaign.

Direct military attack is low likelihood, high consequence. Beijing's direct use of force against Australia or its interests would have significant consequences, but the only likely scenario is the outbreak of a US–China general war.

The challenge that registers as significant in both likelihood and consequence is Beijing's campaign to reshape Southeast Asia. China has consistently signalled that Southeast Asia is a place where it wants to build exclusive influence. Beijing has formidable advantages in the region: the scale of its economy; its considerable infrastructure and advanced technology capabilities; its surging military might; and its willingness to back incumbent regimes, regardless of their records. And were Beijing to persuade Southeast Asian states to become hostile to Australia and its interests, the effects would be debilitating. While not ignoring the other three threats, this is the challenge on which Australia should focus.

Instead, Canberra's approach to China echoes, mimics, supports – choose your word – *follows* US strategy. That strategy has four elements: containment, denial, balancing and deterrence. On *containment*, Australia seeks to frustrate, or at least complicate, China's efforts to build influence, whether through trade and investment, infrastructure or security cooperation. Australian policy-makers speak of providing "alternative options" to Southeast Asian countries. The Albanese government's push to encourage greater trade and investment between Australia and Southeast Asia can be read as a major plank in this effort. The report it commissioned into Australia's trade and investment ties to Southeast Asia by former banker Nicholas Moore paints a rather bleak picture, showing that Australia's trade with the region has plateaued. The proportion of Australia's trade going to Southeast Asia has not grown in fifteen years, despite significant economic growth and trade expansion in the region in that time. It describes Australian investment into Southeast Asia as "underweight," comprising just 3.4 per cent of total Australian international investment. Australia invests more in New Zealand than in Southeast Asia, at a time when the region's share of global foreign investment has more than doubled since the start of the century. With Australia being left in the shade by China, Canada and Japan, the government rightly aims at a step-change in Australia's trade and investment flows with its near north.

Denial involves making China's political and strategic objectives increasingly hard to achieve. The most elaborate exposition of this approach has been developed by Elbridge Colby, under secretary of war for policy in the Trump administration, in his 2021 book, *The Strategy of Denial*. Colby describes an approach in which the United States and its allies judiciously seek to block China from dominating Asia. In frustrating Beijing's ability to achieve its objectives, the strategy of denial aims to provoke China into increasingly coercive means, thus provoking a regional coalition to form in resistance to its designs. The book focuses heavily on Taiwan as Beijing's primary objective, and to a lesser extent the Philippines. The strategy is to harden these countries against Chinese coercion, and Colby is clear about the imperative of binding Australia and Japan to this task. Canberra has willingly responded, integrating its military capabilities and strategic planning ever more deeply with those of its major ally, and, during the Morrison government, talking positively about its willingness to help the US defend Taiwan from a Chinese attack.

Balancing involves assembling a coalition of states opposed to Chinese primacy. It is premised on persuading the bulk of Southeast Asian countries of the prospect and danger of Chinese dominance. With varying levels of volume and nuance, Canberra has embarked on a campaign to galvanise our northern neighbours into greater resistance to China's initiatives and incentives. Frequent admonitions to uphold the "international rules-based order" are intended to highlight Beijing's transgressions of laws and norms in the South China Sea and elsewhere. Warnings about China's "debt-trap" diplomacy, entangling developing countries in webs of obligation to Beijing through the BRI and other initiatives, highlight the coercive intent underlying offers of "win-win cooperation." Canberra's ostentatious blocking of Chinese companies from its telecommunications infrastructure, and its foreign interference laws, are intended to alert others to Beijing's subversive capabilities and intent.

Deterrence seeks to convince China that the costs of resorting to force far outweigh the benefits. It involves Australia's military in the elaborate balance of offensive and defensive manoeuvre as China and the United States each position forces across the region. Particularly since the turn of the century, China has been deploying advanced weapons systems that place at risk US naval forces in the Western Pacific. In response, Australia has agreed to host more US forces on its territory, moving them further away from China's missile batteries and air power, while positioning them closer to the chokepoints through which China's energy supplies flow. And Canberra's bid to acquire nuclear-powered submarines gives it the capacity to contribute to allied operations in order to constrain the Chinese navy's ability to range into the Pacific Ocean.

In following America's approach to the China challenge, Australian strategy has become detached from addressing the most direct threats to our own interests. The focus on defending US power in Northeast Asia, and Taiwan, distracts Australia from the priority threat – a Beijing-led Sphere of Deference in Southeast Asia. Depending on how the denial and deterrence strategies are implemented – and this will be decided in Washington with vanishingly little input by Canberra – they could actually increase the likelihood of a US–China war. Balancing – the effort to convince Southeast Asian states that they need to join a US-led coalition against China – has not worked and will not work. Indonesia, Malaysia, Thailand and Vietnam have shown no interest in joining such a coalition. The Philippines is preoccupied with protecting its territorial waters from Chinese incursion. Vietnam has fraternal communist linkages with Beijing, as well as a common fear of Western-inspired regime change. Hanoi's memory of the huge costs of its alignments during the Indochina wars that raged between 1946 and 1989 makes it very wary of treading a similar path again. Indonesia, Malaysia and Thailand value their economic linkages to China too much to join a countering coalition.

Containment – attempting to complicate Beijing's strategies for achieving exclusive influence and dominance in Southeast Asia – is the only element in Australia's strategy that directly addresses the most significant challenge to our national interests. By giving more resources to a single Office of Southeast Asia, following the Moore report, the government has partially recognised this. But these measures are not sufficient; what is needed is a whole-of-nation approach. Not only trade and diplomacy, but development and defence need to be stitched into an approach with clear strategic objectives and measures. Australia's other advantages, from science and technology to popular culture and higher education, should also be harnessed to the effort. We must become more knowledgeable about our northern neighbours to understand how best to target our efforts. And our policy-makers must recognise that Australia's close identification with US strategy to balance and deter China is a drag on influence and acceptance among our neighbours.

*

There is incomprehension and frustration in Canberra that more countries in Asia do not share our view of the nature of China's power and the threat of its regional dominance. There is even greater perplexity about countries in Southeast Asia that acknowledge in private their misgivings about China's behaviour and intentions but do not follow Australia in making public statements about it or take steps to align diplomatically and militarily with the United States, Australia and Japan. In the region, public trust in China's good intentions is falling. The challenge, as seen from Canberra, is to move

Southeast Asian governments' actions closer to public perceptions. Stated or unstated, directly or indirectly, this is the prism through which Australian diplomacy is conducted.

From Southeast Asian perspectives, the incomprehension is mutual. Privately, government leaders and senior officials in Southeast Asia reacted with shock and disbelief at Australia's ostentatiously confrontational attitude towards China. Many had spent their careers watching Australian governments evolve a pragmatic approach to Beijing that looked very much like their own. Howard's formula of building on shared interests while being mutually respectful of differences had a comfortable ring to it in Jakarta, Singapore, Kuala Lumpur and Bangkok. But as Australian denunciations of China's behaviour in the South China Sea became more strident, as Australian leaders from Kevin Rudd to Julie Bishop took it upon themselves to lecture China on its political values, and as public debate in Australia gravitated towards a monochrome view of a China threat and spoke openly about the drums of war, Southeast Asian policy-makers began to be convinced that Australia had lost the plot. If the intention in Canberra was to provoke a harsh reaction to demonstrate Beijing's coercive tendencies, in Southeast Asian eyes it was a pointless exercise. Few in the region have any illusions about China's capabilities, sensitivities and willingness to bully smaller countries. That is precisely why they avoid provoking Beijing whenever possible, and that is precisely why, when they make decisions that Beijing does not favour, they do so in a very low-key way. Some of the sharper conversations one has in Southeast Asia involve being told that there was little sympathy for Australia in facing Chinese economic coercion, because through its reckless provocations Australia had brought retribution on itself.

When Australian leaders and officials slip into didactic mode with their Southeast Asian counterparts, another common reaction is irritation bordering on resentment. Many note a patronising quality to Australian entreaties, a sense that Australian perceptions of China are clearer and more hard-headed than their regional counterparts'. A former Indonesian ambassador to Australia angrily remarked in private some years ago, "How dare they [in Canberra] tell us how to deal with China? They've been doing this for decades; we've been doing it for centuries." There needs to be greater acknowledgement that Australian perceptions of the China challenge are different from Indonesian, Malaysian, Thai or Singaporean perceptions. While there is concern about China's rise and presence, these countries do not see it as the only source of danger; several see the United States as a strategic concern also. There are occasional charges of hypocrisy, too: Canberra's warnings about becoming too deeply involved in China's Belt and Road Initiative sit incongruously with Australia's willingness to maintain its own vigorous trade relationship with China.

Australia's ever-growing adherence to the American strategy is causing genuine alarm in Southeast Asia. Initiatives intended to balance and deter China are widely viewed as dangerously drawing the region towards an unnecessary war. Had the Australian government been more attentive to long-held views and attitudes among its northern neighbours, the reactions to the AUKUS announcement should have been entirely predictable. Indonesia was "deeply concerned over the continuing arms race and power projection in the region," urging Canberra to "maintain its commitment to regional peace, stability and security." President Joko Widodo was reported to have objected to AUKUS repeatedly and forcefully during a 2021 ASEAN meeting. Malaysian leaders raised concerns that AUKUS could provoke a regional arms race. Less direct than its neighbours but alluding to the same concern with an increasing risk of conflict, Singapore admonished Australia to make sure that AUKUS "would contribute constructively to the peace and stability of the region." The secretive negotiation and sudden announcement of AUKUS also raised concerns in a region that values predictability and consultation. Indonesia was particularly exercised about the circumstances under which Australian nuclear-powered submarines would traverse Indonesian territorial waters. As Southeast Asia analyst Susannah Patton put it, "The concern in Indonesia is not so much that nuclear-powered submarines would be used against it, but that it may be drawn into a conflict by virtue of its archipelagic geography." Against the background of these concerns, one can imagine how Defence Minister Dutton and a top official talking up the prospect of war in Asia was received in Southeast Asia's capitals.

Australia's China-threat foreign policy and its ever-closer adherence to US strategy to counter China are eroding its credibility with the governments in the region of utmost importance to its future. Canberra's wilful self-harm has provided Beijing with a chance to further its case for Asians managing Asian security. China has accused Australia of operating according to a "Cold War mindset," seeking to divide the region and increasing military tensions. This plays directly into historical and contemporary anxieties in Southeast Asia about unwillingly becoming a cockpit for great-power rivalry and conflict. The increased presence of US forces and capabilities on Australian territory is viewed as bringing the possibility of great-power conflict much closer to Southeast Asia. Equally damaging to Australia's interests is that it risks being seen by its neighbours as a spear-carrier for US policy – a particularly dangerous perception at a time when US policy is increasingly unpredictable and unapologetically transactional and self-interested.

Australia seems to have trapped itself in a damaging dynamic. Anxious that it is becoming estranged from its northern neighbours, it makes frenetic efforts to close the growing gap: trade agreements, strategic partnerships, military exercises, annual dialogues, people-to-people initiatives. But at the same time its totalising focus on the China threat and growing integration with US strategy means that none of this activity bridges the underlying divide in geopolitical interests and perceptions. The Indonesian scholar Evan Laksmana warns Australian officials against interpreting strong defence ties between Canberra and Jakarta "as meaning that its strategic outlook will converge with Indonesia's" – a sobering reminder as Prime Minister Albanese inks a new defence agreement with Indonesia. The danger of wishful thinking is indeed acute: ignoring the underlying reality of Australia's strategic drift away from Southeast Asia by focusing on positive statements and shiny agreements in an era of rising tensions.

The Australia I grew up in prospered in a world that fostered its aspirations and strengths. It was a world in which Australia could have an expansive outlook, an ambitious vision of itself and its international preferences. It was a world conducive to small, wealthy, developed states because it was structured around institutions and processes that encouraged countries like Australia to leverage their limited capabilities to achieve outsize influence. These institutions and processes were, first, multilateral bodies that were taken seriously and provided smaller states with a voice and opportunities to join together to advocate major change. Second, a global system of alliances centred on America, dedicated to the values that animate Australia and to ordering the world according to those values. Third, a global economy oriented towards the freest possible flows of goods, investment and technologies, giving us access to markets with strong demand for what we were best at producing, and providing us with the best available products that we didn't produce. Fourth, we abutted a region of states dedicated to pragmatic stability and mutually beneficial economic development and which shared our devotion to the sovereignty and equality of states.

It was a world that encouraged us to be ambitious for a time, but it also allowed us to become complacent. There were several aspects to our complacency. One was an assumption that the four foundational arrangements of the post–World War II order – multilateralism, alliances, globalisation and a benign region – were permanent fixtures, destined to be enduring because – surely – all states judged them to be as beneficial as Australia did. Another aspect of our complacency was an expectation that Australia didn't have to try too hard to secure its interests, because whether we put in the diplomatic effort or not, things just seemed to work out for the best for us. A third aspect was growing indiscipline in being able to specify and prioritise our fundamental national interests. Being Australia, as Howard used to say, meant not having to choose. A fourth aspect was a rising incuriousness about the societies and cultures closest to us geographically. The states in our region appeared to be so stable and predictable as to seem boring; the temptation to take them for granted became overwhelming.

To an Australia shaped by seven decades of living in a world that seemed custom-made in its favour, the last decade and a half has come as a rude shock. The authority and effectiveness of multilateral institutions have been eroded. In recent years, American alliances appear to many states as less about order promotion and more about delivering on the increasingly erratic mood swings occurring in Washington. In Trump's two terms, the value of security partnerships has been questioned by both the United States and its allies. And now we watch the astonishing spectacle of the US threatening a NATO ally with force to acquire Greenland. Globalisation has succumbed to rising economic competitiveness among states and the increasing use of economic interdependence and technology systems as coercive levers. The world isn't deglobalising, but it is fracturing. And the formerly benign region next to Australia has become subject to much greater contestation. For the first time since the end of World War II, a resident Asian power is making a serious bid to develop a sphere of interest right on Australia's doorstep.

So sudden and simultaneous was the crumbling of these four verities of Australia's preferred international order that they exposed how degraded our disciplines for understanding and responding to rapid international change had become. When it became clear that Australia's economic interests and security interests were in serious tension, there was no authoritative mechanism with which to think through what this meant and formulate a new way forward. Reportedly, the Rudd government developed a comprehensive China strategy, but its effects were not apparent, as our relationship with China lurched between confrontation and stand-off in those years. The lack of any coordination was laid bare in 2016, as the economic ministries and security agencies remained fundamentally divided on whether Australia should join the China-initiated AIIB; in the end there was a messy and contested compromise through cabinet. In the absence of discipline and clear and authoritative processes, a combination of alarmism and careerism crept in and came to dominate our foreign, economic and security policy-making. Hyping up the China threat served several objectives: providing a Churchillian sense of moral clarity; reassuring our ally of our loyalty; and providing impetus for rethinking the world in the familiar Manichean terms of democracy versus autocracy.

At no stage did any government between 2007 and the present think through clearly and systematically what all of this change means for Australia's fundamental national interests. Our prime ministerial revolving door didn't help. Instead, Australia seems to have continued along blithely with an expansive internationalist approach that it developed during an earlier, more benign era. At a time of rising challenges in Southeast Asia, Australia developed a close interest in securing a seat on the UN Security Council, holding Russia to account for its attack on a civilian airliner, and pressing for an international inquiry into the origins of Covid-19. Moreover, our leaders seemed to believe that whatever the challenge, the solution was investing ever more heavily in the alliance with the United States. Little thought was given to whether Washington shared our interests, because over time we have simply adopted America's priorities. It is not apparent that Canberra has thought as profoundly as America's European allies have about what the rise of Donald Trump and the movement he represents means for the future of America's role in the world, and therefore for the future of the US–Australia alliance.

We have, in effect, placed all our chips on a single bet: that the US and its strategy for facing down China will protect Australia's interests wherever they are threatened. We seem to be telling ourselves: as long as the United States, Japan and Australia can frustrate Beijing's desire to take over Taiwan, the rest of our interests will be secure. There is more than an element of the old forward defence thinking here: the further from Australia we can take on China, the less likely the problem is to manifest much closer to Australian territory. If this is the thinking in Canberra, it reflects a profound misunderstanding of the scale and nature of China's power. More than a decade into Xi's tenure, it is clear that while Taiwan is a priority for Beijing, it is by no means the only focus. Whether or not it is advancing its objectives in Taiwan, China is assiduously increasing its influence in Southeast Asia, Central Asia, the Pacific, Africa and Latin America. And Washington is not interested in contesting China's influence in any of those regions except – recently – the last.

I have argued that by far the most serious challenge to Australia's interests is the prospect of China developing a Sphere of Deference in Southeast Asia. In support of its efforts, Beijing has formidable advantages and has registered clear intent. Canberra should be in no doubt about this. It is also clear that this danger does not feature on Washington's threat register. Its attention is further north, on the direct threat posed to US bases in Japan, South Korea and Guam by China's asymmetric warfare capabilities. American planners are also intensely focused on developing responses to Chinese coercion against Taiwan. If our major ally really was concerned about China building a Sphere of Deference in Southeast Asia (as arguably it should be), it would have invested in a much more deep and sustained way in building up its commitments and credibility there. Instead, as we've seen, these have been eroding steadily since the end of the Cold War.

*

It should be clear that Australia has made the wrong bet: that relying on the US alliance to address the threat of a Chinese-centred Sphere of Deference on its northern doorstep has left it dangerously exposed and unprepared. If anything, Canberra's adherence to the US strategy of balancing and deterring China has led to an increasing divergence of interests and perceptions between Australia and its neighbours. Furthermore, Australia is unwittingly playing into Beijing's hands. Canberra's championing of AUKUS and the increasing tendency for Australians to view the world as democracies versus authoritarian states have allowed Beijing to argue to Southeast Asians that Western states are confrontational and not to be trusted. As a consequence, Australia is arguably at an all-time low in its ability to shape events and attitudes in Southeast Asia, precisely when it needs to have maximum influence and legitimacy.

This should be a time in which we start to recalibrate and think about our interests and the real challenges to them. Our tendency to ally with a culturally familiar great power for our entire history as a nation has left us in a state of perpetual strategic adolescence, all too willing to take direction, originally from Whitehall and now from Washington, about where our real interests lie and how we should act to further them. The first step of our strategic maturation has to be to understand that our fundamental national interests are not congruent with America's. We have an interest in the United States remaining anchored in the Pacific through its Northeast Asian bases, but this is not Australia's only, or even our primary, interest. Our primary interest must be to work to prevent China building a Sphere of Deference on our northern doorstep. We must be very clear that our alliance will only be marginally helpful in this task, and as currently constituted to confront China directly it is downright unhelpful. The ultimate act of achieving greater strategic maturity can only occur when we realise that we must be self-reliant in our thinking about our interests and our fate.

There are four steps Australia needs to take to address the real and present danger to its national interests in Southeast Asia. The first is to understand the scale of the challenge, and match objectives with available means. It means we must think about the different arms of Australia's statecraft – diplomacy, development assistance, defence capabilities and institutional membership – and what is the best combination of these to achieve our objectives. As we become more self-reliant, we will quickly realise we have underinvested in diplomacy and development and focused our defence spending on capabilities that are more aligned with our ally's needs than our own.

The second step is fundamentally to change the way we think about our alliance with the United States. We need to stop thinking about it as an *end* of Australian foreign policy – meaning that we structure our diplomatic and security actions with the goal of building ever closer engagement with the US – and return to thinking about it as a *means*. We need to be more clear-eyed about where, when and how the alliance contributes to our interests and objectives. And we need to be clear about standing firm against the inevitable American pressure for us to overinvest in the alliance. This will involve having the confidence that the alliance continues to be important to the US; its intelligence stations on our soil are too important to its global intelligence and military posture to walk away from. Yes – we can say no to Washington and maintain the alliance.

The third step is to start looking at Southeast Asia not in instrumental terms, as a means to achieving larger interests, but on its own terms. This means looking past strategically meaningless bromides like the "Indo-Pacific" and thinking about actual strategic geography. Australia needs to invest heavily in deepening its understanding of the countries to our north; invest in the skills of geopolitical empathy. This means sustained effort to understand the complex mix of historical conditions and contemporary preoccupations that shape how these countries relate to each other and to countries outside of their immediate zone. We must build a clear and nuanced understanding of the frameworks through which our counterparts in Jakarta, Singapore, Putrajaya, Bangkok, Hanoi and Manila think about the world. For our diplomats in those capitals, it means seldom talking and mainly listening.

Fourth is to increase our maturity in how we deal with new challenges and threats. I hope the last decade, in which Australia lost all perspective in reacting to the China threat, will be remembered as a salutary lesson in how not to react to new challenges. There will be more strategic shocks coming that we will need to understand and process; the crumbling of the four pillars of our familiar world guarantees that. What is needed is a new discipline in assessing challenges and thinking rigorously about their likelihood and consequences. Urgently, we need to build greater contestability into our assessment and policy processes, reversing the monocular culture that has overgrown the system over the last decade.

I am anticipating an avalanche of negative responses to my arguments, ranging from derision to horror. I fear we have sleepwalked into a mindset in which to think more independently of the United States, and to consider the alliance as one of the means of our foreign policy rather as the end of it, is literally unthinkable. If this is the case, we are undergoing not a process of strategic maturation, but one of strategic infantilisation. We need to remember an earlier period in Australia, between 1975 and 2005, when we became more self-reliant in thinking about a rapidly shifting geopolitical landscape in Asia. That was an era in which we planned for much greater defence self-reliance and integrated our regional diplomacy and development policy with this aim. Arguably, it was the period when we reached the pinnacle of our understanding of and influence in Southeast Asia. Greater self-reliance and greater influence on our immediate north are not just correlated; they are interdependent.

*

Australia's immediate priority must be to refocus attention on our greatest strategic challenge: the possibility that China will succeed in building a Sphere of Deference in Southeast Asia. This is not contingent on the US–China contest in Northeast Asia; it is a campaign that is already well underway and will continue irrespective of the dynamics of Sino–US rivalry, short of the outbreak of war. In a nutshell, Australia's priority must be to work with Southeast Asia's states to ensure that they do not succumb to incorporation in a Chinese sphere of interest. This requires a diplomacy very different from a didactic approach that constantly warns of the China threat and encourages our neighbours to muscle up to Beijing. It should begin by understanding and acknowledging Southeast Asian states' perceptions of the China challenge, and their parameters and preferences for dealing with it. And it needs to be underpinned by a strong understanding of the incentives and fears that animate Southeast Asia's own internal relations.

Australia should be prepared to work with Southeast Asia's strong resistance to being folded into Beijing's hierarchic order. This has many aspects. Among these states is a fundamental adherence to the principle of the sovereign rights and equality of all states, irrespective of size, which has led and will continue to lead to extreme aversion to any suggestion that they are of secondary status or incidental to larger designs. Second, ASEAN has norms of non-interference, the non-use of force, mutual deference, consultation and consensus. China contravenes these norms weekly in the South China Sea, and the result has been a steady rise in distrust. Another element is the fraught politics of Chinese-ness within and between the region's three core states, Indonesia, Malaysia and Singapore. Any shift in the region's relationship to China is likely to perturb the central tension in the region's core, and so will be approached with extreme wariness. Fourth, the Chinese bid for regional leadership will grate with those countries that have leadership designs themselves: particularly Indonesia, but also Malaysia and Thailand. Encouraging their leadership visions will be a very handy block to China's ambitions. Fifth, it is becoming clearer that China's offer of win-win economic integration with Southeast Asia has less to recommend it in practice, particularly as its economy is revealed to be more competitive than complementary with its southern neighbours, and as China's exports to the region threaten the manufacturing sector there.

Australia should take comfort from each of these factors and be prepared to work with them. Ultimately, China offers Southeast Asia a choice just as binary as that offered by the United States and its allies: align with China against the West. Beijing appears not to understand that a commitment not to make binary choices is a deeply ingrained norm in Southeast Asia; indeed, the act of not choosing is seen as the ultimate act of agency and autonomy. The tradition of non-alignment in Southeast Asia is evolving into a preference for omni-engagement: encouraging a range of external powers to engage with the region and balance each other's influence. This is ultimately what is behind Indonesia joining the BRICS group of states and Malaysia and Thailand becoming BRICS partners; rather than signalling gravitation away from the West, it shows they are seeking to balance China's power by engaging with India and Russia.

China's ability to persuade its southern neighbours to join a Sphere of Deference will depend on convincing them that the benefits are greater than the risks. Ultimately, Beijing will need to rely on persuasion, because geography prevents it from exercising the type of military coercion that Russia and the United States are currently exercising in their spheres of interest. China cannot afford to fail in Southeast Asia by becoming too coercive; it remembers Vietnam's long isolation by ASEAN after it used force against its neighbours. This will lend a particular caution to Beijing's actions in relation to its putative hinterland.

Australia's ideal outcome will be a region in which China is engaged but not dominant. Most Southeast Asian states already defer to Beijing's wishes, with Indonesia, Malaysia and Brunei electing to remain silent on the treatment of Muslims in Xinjiang, and Malaysia and Indonesia keeping their counsel on Beijing's claims in the South China Sea. The question is where the limits of their deference lie. If Southeast Asia's core and first-tier states continue to remain stubbornly independent in protecting their core national interests – their freedom to engage with multiple partners and institutions – this is a world that Australia can very much live with. Because that is a region with which Australia can build enduring ties and alignments, and which cannot be used by Beijing to pressure Australia.

All of this is a very long way from where we are today. It involves moving from viewing Southeast Asia through a China lens to viewing China through a Southeast Asia lens – and not an America lens. This is a profound change in perspective. It will require Australia to acquire a level of self-confidence in dealing with China that its Southeast Asian neighbours have. It will require having the humility to watch and learn from how our northern neighbours deal with the Chinese behemoth. It will require a new journey of strategic maturation.

NOTES

2 Churchill argued: Bob Wurth, *The Battle for Australia: A nation and its leader under siege*, Macmillan, 2013.

4 These fears: Neville Meaney, *The Search for Security in the Pacific*, University of Sydney Press, 1976.

4 "flexible tripwire": Bruce Hunt, *Australia's Northern Shield? Papua New Guinea and the defence of Australia since 1980*, Monash University Publishing, 2017.

4 "To exert": Memo from R.N. Hamilton to James Plimsoll, Department of External Affairs, quoted in David Goldsworthy, *Losing the Blanket: Australia and the end of Britain's empire*, Melbourne University Press, 2002, p. 51.

5 "safeguarding Australia's interests": Australian Government, *National Defence Strategy*, Canberra, 2024.

6 "The outsized influence": United States Government, *National Security Strategy of the United States of America*, Washington, DC, November 2025.

6 "we live in a world": Stephen Miller, interview with Jake Tapper, CNN, 5 January 2026.

13 From 1946: Stephan Frühling, *A History of Australian Strategic Policy since 1945*, Canberra, Commonwealth of Australia, 2009.

14 "which most substantially engage": Australian Government, *In the National Interest*, Canberra, Commonwealth of Australia, 1997, p. 57.

14 adds the Republic of Korea: Australian Government, *Advancing the National Interest*, Canberra, Commonwealth of Australia, 2003, pp. 77–83.

14 "lift the ambition": Australian Government, *2017 Foreign Policy White Paper*, Canberra, 2017, pp. 37–43.

14 sits within a broader strategic realm: My thanks to Peter Varghese for this observation. Personal correspondence, 26 January 2026.

16 most vigorous trading region on Earth: Anthony Reid, *Southeast Asia in the Age of Commerce, 1450–1680*, New Haven, Yale University Press, 1988.

16 This trading history: Nicholas Tarling, *Nations and States in Southeast Asia*, Cambridge University Press, 1998.

17 surpassed or suppressed: Anthony Milner, *The Malays*, Wiley-Blackwell, 2007.

17 states divided: Tony Day, *Fluid Iron: State formation in Southeast Asia*, University of Hawaii Press, 2002.

17 a sense of shared vulnerability: Amitav Acharya, *The Making of Southeast Asia: International relations of a region*, Institute of Southeast Asian Studies, 2013.

18 a sense of the regional interest: Amitav Acharya, *Constructing a Security Community in Southeast Asia*, Routledge, 2014.

18 threaten to upset: John Ciorciari, *The Limits of Alignment: Southeast Asia and the great powers since 1945*, Georgetown University Press, 2010.

19 triangular relationship between Indonesia, Malaysia and Singapore: Southeast Asia scholar Lily Rahim refers to these three states as Southeast Asia's security, economic and intellectual core. Lily Rahim, *Singapore in the Malay World*, Routledge, 2009.

19 Indonesia and Malaysia combine: Joseph Liow, *The Politics of Indonesia–Malaysia Relations*, RoutledgeCurzon, 2005.

24 "Southeast Asia has since": Speech by Chinese president Xi Jinping to the Indonesian Parliament, 3 October 2013.

25 Imperial China's international relations: John Fairbank, *The Chinese World Order*, Harvard University Press, 1968.

25 The sense that ethnic Chinese: Stephen FitzGerald, *China and the Overseas Chinese*, Cambridge University Press, 1972.

26 30 million people of Chinese descent: Taiwan Overseas Community Affairs Council, *Statistical Yearbook*, Taipei, 2024.

29 18 per cent increase: Sam Harwick, "Asia responds to a leaderless trading system", *East Asia Forum*, July–September 2025.

29 willing integration of China's economy: Selina Ho and Terence Lee, "Elite perceptions of a China-led regional order in Southeast Asia", *Journal of Current Southeast Asian Affairs*, vol. 44, no. 1, 2025, pp. 148–73.

29 few doubt: Ho and Lee, "Elite perceptions of a China-led regional order."

29 Southeast Asians' trust: Lee Sue-Ann and William Choong, "Southeast Asian perceptions of China: Beijing's growing power is recognised, but feared", *ISEAS Perspective*, no. 46, 18 June 2024.

29 creates a confidence: Timothy Heath, *China's New Governing Party Paradigm*, Routledge, 2014.

30 "for the people of Asia": Eugene Tan and Lye Liang Fook, "Assessing China's call for 'strategic autonomy' in Southeast Asia", *ISEAS Perspective*, 17 March 2025.

31 three propositions: Chin-Hao Huang, "China's role in Southeast Asia in 2021", *Southeast Asian Affairs*, vol. 2022, 2022, pp. 60–72.

31 Australia needs to think: Jennifer Lind, "Life in China's Asia: What regional hegemony would look like", *Foreign Affairs*, vol. 97, no. 2, March–April 2018.

33 America was vulnerable: A.T. Mahan, *The Problem of Asia*, Boston, Little, Brown and Company, 1900.

33 From ports: Michael Green, *By More than Providence: Grand strategy and American power in the Pacific since 1783*, Columbia University Press, 2017.

35 advocating for an Australian version of the Monroe Doctrine: Roger Thompson, *Australian Imperialism in the Pacific*, Melbourne University Press, 1980.

35 US security guarantee: W. David MacIntyre, *Background to the ANZUS Pact*, St Martin's Press, 1995.

36 chain of falling dominoes: Peter Edwards, *Australia and the Vietnam War*, NewSouth Books, 2014.

36 "Australia could well": Frühling, *A History of Australian Strategic Policy Since 1945*, p. 20.

37 Washington suspected Canberra: Gareth Evans, *Incorrigible Optimist: A political memoir*, Melbourne University Press, 2017.

37 They could benefit: Joseph Liow, *Ambivalent Engagement: The United States and regional security in Southeast Asia after the Cold War*, Brookings Institution Press, 2017.

37 American covert intervention: Audrey Kahin and George Kahin, *Subversion as Foreign Policy: The secret Eisenhower and Dulles debacle in Indonesia*, New York, The New Press, 1995.

38 bringing together such erstwhile rivals: Michael Barr, *Cultural Politics and Asian Values*, RoutledgeCurzon, 2002.

40 "responsible stakeholder": Robert Zoellick, "Whither China? From membership to responsibility", Remarks to the National Committee on US–China Relations, New York, 21 September 2005.

44 Alliances shift: United States Government, *National Security Strategy of the United States of America*, Washington, DC, November 2025.

48–9 The relationship between Australia and China: John Howard, Address to a Dinner in Honour of His Excellency Mr Li Peng, Canberra, 17 September 2002.

50 "Western countries see": Kevin Rudd, *On Xi Jinping*, Oxford University Press, 2024.

50 "wake up to find": Duncan Lewis, quoted in Peter Hartcher, "'Insidious': Former ASIO boss warns on Chinese interference in Australia", *The Sydney Morning Herald*, 22 November 2019.

50 Howard reflected with pride: John Howard, *Lazarus Rising*, HarperCollins, 2010.

51 "economic partnerships": Remarks by US President Barack Obama to the Australian Government, Parliament House, Canberra, 17 November 2011.

51 "deepest complacency": Tony Abbott, quoted in James Curran, "Australia's coronavirus reset: Not time for retreat", *Australian Financial Review*, 3 April 2020.

51 "Australia had been betrayed": James Curran, *Australia's China Odyssey*, NewSouth Books, 2022, p. 251.

53 "Modern China was founded": Malcolm Turnbull, Comments, 9 December 2017.

54 "We need to call them": Curran, *Australia's China Odyssey*, p. 220.

55 A coercive China: Malcolm Turnbull, Keynote Address to the Shangri La Dialogue, 3 June 2017.

56 Canberra's defence agreements: Rahman Yaacob, Susannah Patton and Jack Sato, "Southeast Asia's Evolving Defence Partnerships", Lowy Institute Analysis, 19 August 2025.

56 "dialogue enables": Penny Wong, Remarks to the Australia–China Strategic Dialogue, 20 March 2024.

57 China-watcher Richard McGregor: Richard McGregor, *Xi Jinping: The backlash*, Penguin, 2019.

57 American exporters were direct beneficiaries: James Laurenceson and Thomas Pantle, "Economic reality bites: What Australia needs to know amidst US-China strategic competition", Australia–China Relations Institute online, 30 November 2021.

59 "the most comprehensive punitive trade measures": Richard McGregor, "Chinese coercion, Australian resilience", Lowy Institute Analysis, 20 October 2022.

59 less than 1 per cent of GDP: Naoise McDonagh, "Hidden lessons from China's coercion campaign against Australia, *AIIA Analysis*, 28 February 2024.

59 "It's almost as though": Jamie Seidel, "China's three ships more than a match for Australia's entire navy", News.com.au, 5 December 2025.

62 "underweight": Nicholas Moore, *Invested: Australia's Southeast Asia economic strategy to* 2040, CanPrint Communications, September 2023.

62 Colby is clear: Elbridge A. Colby, *The Strategy of Denial*, New Haven, Yale University Press, 2021, p. 236.

64 We must become more knowledgeable: Garry Rodan, "The new political economy of Australia-Southeast Asia engagement", *Australian Journal of International Affairs*, vol. 79, no. 6, 2025.

66 "deeply concerned": Indonesian Government, Statement on Australia's Nuclear-Powered Submarines Program, 17 September 2021.

66 "would contribute": Singapore Prime Minister Lee Hsien Loong's telephone call with Australian Prime Minister Scott Morrison, 16 September 2021.

66 "The concern in Indonesia": Susannah Patton, "How Southeast Asia views AUKUS", Lowy Institute Commentary, 24 February 2024.

67 "as meaning": Evan Laksmana, "Embracing the different ways Indonesia and Australia view the region", *The Interpreter*, Lowy Institute, 20 April 2023.

Tim Dunlop

Sean Kelly's essay has, through his careful wrestling with the issues, helped clarify my thinking on key issues, and I thank him for it. He has put forth the best account possible, I think, of the argument at the centre of progressive politics, the tension between pragmatism and reaching for the stars – and it deserves a wide audience.

But the battle within Labor that Kelly sets out is lost. After the Bondi terrorist attack, no one can any longer presume that Anthony Albanese is merely a temporarily embarrassed progressive being forced into actions against the better angels of his nature. He is a deeply pragmatic, hard-nosed politician effectively of the centre-right, someone who long ago took the pragmatic side in the battle that Kelly documents.

Kelly frames the central issue precisely towards the end of the essay: "Rather than trying to bring about a better country by constantly avoiding the topics the powerful want us to avoid, a government of the centre-left might consider making those topics its starting point." But that is the whole point. Albanese is not ever going to do that, and he can keep winning elections from now until the turn of next century and we will never again get a Labor government of the centre-left.

Those issues are off the table, by design. That's what Albanese's much-vaunted "incrementalism" amounts to.

As Kelly says, the very idea of "a natural party of government" is deeply conservative and it is telling that the prime minister's most decisive acts have been those within institutional and administrative frames that seek to maintain the status quo: his effective expulsion of Senator Fatima Payman from the party in the name of internal party discipline, and changes to parliamentary staffing levels and campaign finance laws in order to preserve the architecture of the two-party system.

And now we have the new anti-hate legislation, which criminalises acts of protest that were once, at worst, civil matters, bringing a new level of authoritarianism to our politics. Why would we presume Anthony Albanese has taken such steps against his better judgement?

The pragmatic argument is that, somehow, these actions are what "the people" want, but we have reason to doubt this. The people's revealed preferences – through their voting over decades now – is that they are fed up with a two-party system that has drained the nation of its egalitarian ethos. People keep voting against this two-party "settlement," as the most recent Australian Electoral Study shows in some detail. Combined support for the "major" parties now falls below two-thirds, and more people vote for smaller parties and independents than vote for the Liberals. Young voters and women are increasingly withdrawing support from the Coalition, producing a durable generational and gender realignment, though Labor's persistently low primary vote suggests it is not the sole beneficiary of that shift. And we all know about the current surge in the One Nation vote. In short, our governing architecture is built for a two-party system people no longer fully support, and as a democracy we need to accommodate that shift.

Labor, through its multi-decade acquiescence to market economics as the central rationality of its governing posture, and in its incremental submission to years of right-wing culture wars, has turned from being the party of the working class and social progress into some sort of plasticine edifice that events shape at their will. The idea that any sort of progressive outcome is possible under this formation – this party of Albanese with his dream of Labor as the natural party of government – is farcical.

At the same time, the non-Labor side of Australian politics continues to fray in ways that give the lie to the idea that our two-party system is inherently stable. To the extent that there is any party discipline among the Liberals and the Nationals, it is supplied by News Corp, but the truth is even it has very little left to work with at the moment. The deckchairs on the *Titanic* are being rearranged after the ship has sunk.

What we are seeing in Australia at the moment is not so much a collapse of the established political order as its complete realignment. The effect is not chaos but a rapidly emerging authoritarianism spreading across the political landscape, from the far right to the "sensible centre." Once we would've expected Labor to be a bulwark against such developments, but those days are gone, at least for as long as it remains the party of Albanese.

The question for the progressive faction of Australian politics is how it reorganises itself now that Labor can no longer be relied on to lead.

Tim Dunlop

THE GOOD FIGHT

Correspondence

Emma Dawson

Sean Kelly poses a fundamental question in his Quarterly Essay: what do our political leaders believe? It is a question usually absent from Australia's civic conversation, which is dominated by a shallow obsession with the "horse race" of political contest. By contrast, Kelly's reflection on the principles and practice of the Australian Labor Party is thoughtful and nuanced. It is also suffused with frustration about Labor's performance in government since 2022, reflecting an increasingly common view among Australians who are both progressive in outlook and highly engaged with politics: that Albanese is too timid, not ambitious enough for the nation; that he is shirking the great moral responsibility Labor has always carried: "to change things on behalf of those who desperately need them to change."

The reason for Kelly's frustration is articulated towards the end of the essay, where he deftly outlines the global impact of decades of neoliberal economics, which has led to levels of inequality rivalling those of the late nineteenth century in developed nations. At the same time, and not coincidentally, politics has become highly polarised, and society more fractured. The civil unrest in the United States, UK and Europe resembles that of the 1930s, and Australia – long considered safe from the kind of violence that has characterised older nations – has now experienced a devastating, ideologically motivated terrorist attack at Bondi Beach, the very definition of "home soil."

This, Kelly argues, is the time for a bold, left-wing politician to fight for social justice. He is sceptical that Albanese has that "good fight" in him, comparing his approach unfavourably with the grand rhetoric and revolutionary social change of Whitlam and, most damningly, with the "risk that excites" reformist style of the Hawke/Keating years.

Kelly's thesis is that by declaring an ambition to become "the natural party of government" and stating his belief that Labor "stand[s] for the vast majority of interests in this country," Albanese has abandoned Labor's role as the party of reform. His ambition, Kelly suggests, is little more than a cipher for being "all things to all people" and means that the major parties' positions have reversed, with Labor now playing the role of conserving the status quo.

This is where an otherwise excellent essay goes wrong.

Kelly's thesis rests on the idea that the Australian Labor Party identifies itself primarily in opposition to the dominant Liberal–National Coalition – that it is "a party shaped around countering the right." This argument rests on flimsy ground: a claim by historian Brian McKinley that the ALP, in its early years, was little more than "a coalition of disparate elements … linked … by hostility to Australian conservatism." And so, Kelly asks, if Labor is no longer by definition "not the Liberal Party" then just what is the ALP today?

But this definition of Labor is wrong – he has it back to front. Labor is the party against which other movements in Australia are set, not the other way around.

Before World War II, Australia's parliament was populated by members of the Australian Labor Party, which has existed since before Federation, and an ever-changing suite of conservative parties that were, before they had any coherent platform of their own, defined primarily in opposition to Labor. (Indeed, in the weeks since *The Good Fight* was published, this history has been thrown into full view, as the Coalition has separated again into its disparate parts, while other right-wing forces cannibalise conservative voters, and populist politicians begin to break bread with One Nation.)

This fundamental misunderstanding of the ALP undermines Kelly's critique of Albanese and stymies his ability to see clearly what Labor is doing in government. Kelly's failure is to understand the purpose of Labo(u)r as a movement that, as Albanese told the UK Labour Party Conference in September 2025, "chose democracy" as the path to social reform. In fact, the word "purpose" is almost entirely missing from Kelly's essay, when in fact it is purpose rather than belief that drives the labour movement and informs the policies and actions of the Labor government.

From its earliest days among the sheep shearers of Barcaldine and the revolutionaries of the Eureka Stockade, the Australian labour movement was concerned with the quotidian demands of working people. The origins of the Australian Labor Party rest on organised labour and the collective decision to build, from a grassroots movement for workers' rights, a political party that could utilise the power of Parliament: the culmination of a movement that sought not just to protest the laws of the ruling class but to change them.

This origin story is markedly different to that of the lofty idealism of democratic liberalism in the United States that created the Democratic Party from a branch of the Jeffersonian Republicans. There are also key differences in the way

Australian Labor entered electoral politics to the path taken by its British sister party. The ALP was, by virtue of demographics, led determinedly by working people and far less prone to the influence of the Fabian socialism espoused by the Victorian cultural elite.

It is true that Labor is Australia's party of reform. Throughout our history, it has been Labor that has taken the public policy initiatives that shape and define the Australian way of life. From full employment and the creation of a robust welfare state in the postwar years, through the design of the Pharmaceutical Benefits Scheme and our once-world-leading vocational training system, to the establishment of universal healthcare and superannuation, the building of the National Broadband Network and the invention of the National Disability Insurance Scheme – it has been Labor governments that have undertaken the great, nation-building programs that create wealth and wellbeing for the majority of people.

It has done so patiently and methodically: for example, the pursuit of universal healthcare did not start, as Kelly claims, with Whitlam, but with Curtin and Chifley. It took Labor forty years to implement and secure Medicare. This slow and dogged pursuit of reform has always been central to Labor's way of governing.

It is this that Albanese has in mind when he says, "we represent the vast majority of interests in this country": his conviction that, despite decades of social atomisation and economic plunder under increasingly reactionary neoliberal rule, Australians still value the collective achievements that set Australia apart from other established democracies, and the fact that they were achieved through policy and persuasion, with a minimum of social conflict.

For, despite the wailing of the progressive cultural class, Australia is a more left-wing country than most English-speaking democracies, largely by virtue of strong democratic institutions and laws, most often enacted by the ALP. It is not just our universal health and superannuation systems that are the envy of the world: Australia was the first country to establish the concept of a minimum wage, led the world in the achievement of the eight-hour day, and was one of the first countries to legislate equal pay for women. Most young Australians are shocked to hear that it was the Blair Labour government that first legislated a legally binding minimum wage in the UK – in 1999.

Australia's egalitarian culture rests on this history of rights and institutions fought for by, and directed to the welfare of, working people. Albanese understands this history of purpose and, more importantly, knows that the majority of non-Indigenous Australians share a view of the country as one of opportunity. Whether descended from miserable convicts brutalised by the British ruling class or from an immigrant or refugee seeking to build a better life, settler Australia has been a great experiment in genuine freedom for people who started life with little and sought to build security and prosperity through opportunity and effort.

The actions of the Albanese government sit squarely within this traditional purpose of providing and protecting opportunity and ensuring that national prosperity is shared – not through revolutionary means, but by careful reforms enacted through government.

Kelly claims to find the lists of achievements sometimes posted online by supporters of the ALP unconvincing, which is perhaps why he doesn't bother to identify the common purpose behind those achievements. Fair enough: that's really the job of politicians. Yet by focusing on what Labor has done rather than on its rhetorical emphasis on caution and consensus, an astute observer of Albanese's government would recognise a clearly social-democratic program of reform.

Industrial relations changes have been significant and far-reaching: for the first time in a decade, the labour share of national growth is rising and real wages are increasing. Wage increases for essential workers in the care sector are being delivered, as are increased hours of early childhood education and care for children of all backgrounds. Free TAFE is supporting young people to gain useful qualifications that will enable them to pursue careers in a post-carbon Australia. Industry policy is being enacted to create those jobs of the future and decarbonise the economy. Social housing is being built and a vehicle for its long-term funding has been established. Treasury is broadening its scope to consider other measures of wellbeing beyond GDP, and inflation has been reduced without an increase in unemployment. The most egregious abuses of the welfare system are being addressed, not least through the rapid reversal of cuts to single parenting payments in Jim Chalmers' first budget. Young people without the "bank of mum and dad" are being supported into home ownership. The NBN will remain in public ownership. The national electricity grid is being upgraded for renewables and households supported to switch to solar. The destruction of progressive income taxation was reversed, and Australian children are no longer exposed to the manipulative and harmful algorithms of social media platforms. And record investments in Medicare along with the creation of urgent care clinics have begun to restore the promise of universal healthcare that is free at the point of delivery.

Many of the measures implemented qualify as pre- rather than re-distributive and, as such, are clearly labourist in ideology. That is, they are aimed at giving people opportunity and agency in an increasingly unequal world, rather than being satisfied with distributing the spoils of our common wealth through the welfare system.

The policies legislated and implemented since May 2022 have begun to reverse the more damaging effects of the neoliberal economic order, but the challenge of creating a new structure to replace it is a long-term project.

Albanese surely knows this and is cognisant that Labor is in power at a time of real social and economic disruption across the world, one not seen for almost a century. It is in this context that he seeks to govern cautiously and inclusively, listening to all Australians, not just the loudest voices from right and left.

Keating's "risk that excites" may appeal to progressives who live comfortable lives, but risk is only exciting to those who either can afford to take it or have nothing to lose if it fails. Most Australians in 2026 are wary of risk, and of politicians who promise – or threaten – big change. Unlike the hollowed-out working classes in the north of England or America's rural south, Australian working people still have something – largely thanks to Labor's efforts to ameliorate the worst effects of neoliberalism in the 1980s – to lose. They have voted for change, but to proceed with caution. Albanese is heeding their call.

Emma Dawson

THE GOOD FIGHT

Correspondence

Kos Samaras

Sean Kelly's *The Good Fight* arrives at a moment when Australian politics feels simultaneously frozen and volatile, a curious condition that his analysis helps explain, even if his diagnosis requires extension. Kelly's central argument is that Labor has become what conservatives once were: proud defenders of the status quo. This is a failure of imagination and courage, he suggests, at precisely the moment when boldness is required. It is a sharp critique, sympathetically rendered by a former Labor staffer who clearly wants the party to succeed. But I want to push Kelly's analysis further, into territory he identifies but which is not fully part of the scope of his essay.

Kelly captures something important about the Albanese government's political style. The prime minister, speaking to what Kelly describes as a fragmented and disengaged electorate, places a high value on moderation. This often means ducking fights with entrenched interests – on negative gearing, on capital gains tax, on fossil-fuel exports. The result, Kelly argues, risks embedding an ever more unequal nation, led by a government that can seem gutless. He quotes Paul Keating's formulation that leadership requires imagination and courage, and clearly fears Albanese falls short on both counts.

Yet Kelly also finds reasons for cautious optimism. He credits the government with gradually dismantling two key national assumptions: the centrality of the US alliance and the attitudes and assumptions of neoliberalism. And he suggests that the end of ideology may yet offer hope for a new politics. This is where I part company with Kelly, not because he is wrong about what is happening but because I think he underestimates the danger of what happens if Labor fails to act on the opening he identifies.

Kelly frames the problem as one of political will. I want to reframe it as one of structural obsolescence.

Labor's historical mission was built around what I would call a compact between capital, labour and the state. The terms were straightforward: growth would be generated, and Labor's job was to ensure workers received their fair share through wages, conditions and the social wage of public services. For generations, this worked. Even when Labor lost elections, the underlying settlement remained intact. Howard could win four terms while maintaining Medicare, increasing the pension and presiding over a wages boom. The compact held.

What Kelly describes as the exhaustion of neoliberalism is, I would argue, the collapse of this compact. The majority of Australians no longer experience the economy as a system that rewards their contribution. They experience it as a system that extracts from them while rewarding those who already possess assets, credentials or connections. Qualitative research conducted by RedBridge Group throughout 2025, across diverse Australian communities, reveals a nation experiencing profound economic anxiety, institutional distrust and generational fracture. This is not partisan disaffection. This is a comprehensive loss of faith in the mechanisms that were supposed to translate economic participation into economic security.

The image accompanying this reflection, drawn from that research synthesis, describes Australia's social fabric as strained but not broken, anxious but not without hope. That formulation matters. Australians have not become atomised consumers incapable of solidarity. They retain strong instincts towards fairness, mutual obligation and collective provision. What they lack is a political vehicle that speaks to these instincts with a program adequate to the moment.

This is where Kelly's critique and my structural analysis converge. If Labor's task, historically, has been to change things on behalf of those who desperately need them to change, then defending the status quo is not merely insufficient, it is a betrayal of purpose. But the danger runs deeper than Kelly acknowledges. A party that appears to defend a broken settlement does not simply fail to inspire. It actively alienates those who have correctly diagnosed that the settlement no longer serves them.

Here we arrive at a phenomenon that should alarm Labor strategists far more than it apparently does: the collapse of the Liberal Party's working-class base into the arms of One Nation. This is not merely a Coalition problem. It is a warning about what happens when a political party's traditional constituency concludes that their vehicle can no longer deliver.

For decades, working-class conservatives voted Liberal on the promise of aspiration, the compact from the other direction, where economic growth would create opportunity for those willing to work. That promise has curdled just as thoroughly as Labor's version. Housing is unattainable. Job security has evaporated. The wages of work no longer purchase the life that work was supposed to provide. The Liberal Party's response has been to double down on culture war grievances precisely because it has nothing material to offer. And a significant portion of their former base has responded by abandoning them, not because One Nation has a credible economic program but because grievance politics at least acknowledges that something has gone wrong, even if its diagnosis is false and its prescriptions are worse.

Labor may continue to defeat this hollowed-out Coalition. Kelly is right that Albanese's moderation appeals to large numbers of Australians, as it did in the 2025 election. But victory over a collapsing opponent is not the same as building durable support. If Labor cannot offer a program that matches the scale of economic transformation required, if it continues to appear as the defender of arrangements that no longer deliver, its own working-class and younger voters will eventually seek vehicles that at least promise to try.

Kelly's essay is, ultimately, a call for Labor to find its courage. I am suggesting the stakes are higher than even that framing implies. The compact is broken, but the desire for a compact endures. Australians want to believe that work should provide security, that the next generation should do better than the last, that public institutions should serve the public. They have not abandoned these values; they have simply lost faith that any party can deliver them.

Kelly identifies Labor's gradual retreat from neoliberal assumptions as grounds for hope. I would argue it is necessary but nowhere near sufficient. The question is not whether Labor can slowly dismantle old orthodoxies while maintaining broad appeal. It is whether slow dismantling can outpace the erosion of faith in the political system itself. The working-class voters who have fled the Liberals for One Nation are not patient reformers. They are people who have given up on the major parties as vehicles for their economic interests and now vote primarily on grievance and identity.

This is the fate that awaits Labor if Kelly's warning goes unheeded: not defeat at the hands of the Coalition, but slow-motion irrelevance as the party that managed decline while claiming to stand for something more. The social fabric remains capable of bearing weight. Whether Labor proves capable of weaving something new from it remains, as Kelly makes clear, genuinely uncertain.

Kos Samaras

THE GOOD FIGHT

Correspondence

John Quiggin

Reading Sean Kelly's *The Good Fight*, I was struck by an observation attributed to John Howard: "in the 1960s, he said, 40 per cent reliably voted Labor, 40 per cent Liberal, with 20 per cent in the centre. The proportion of swing voters, he said, had doubled since then."

As regards the 1960s, Howard was broadly accurate, except for omitting the role of the Democratic Labour Party, which eventually served as a waystation for conservative Catholics moving from Labor to the Liberals. At the time, a lot of commentary treated the swinging voters as making considered decisions and compared them favourably to those who always voted the same way. But more careful analysis undertaken by Rod Cameron for Labor in the 1980s and cited by Stephen Mills in *The New Machine Men* showed that swing voters did not carefully reason their way to a vote. Rather, "They are basically ignorant and indifferent about politics, voting for ... superficial, ill-informed and generally selfish reasons." On the other hand, as Associate Professor Sally Young wrote in 2013, "those who know the most about politics and are most interested in it, are usually partisan. Much like sports fans, they've picked a side."

Back in the 1960s, the "sports fan" analogy told part of the story, but only part. The parties weren't just competing teams (routine use of this term to describe a party's representatives came much later). Rather, the parties embodied different views of which voters were truly representative of Australia and advocated very different policies as a result. For Labor, the representative group was the working class, epitomised by unionised manual workers. For the anti-Labor parties, it was Menzies' "forgotten people" (educated professionals and small business owners), along with the rural voters represented by the Country Party (now the Nationals).

So the archetypal voter for each party not only identified with that party but saw themselves reflected in the party's rhetoric and policies. In particular, Labor favoured pro-union industrial relations policies, progressive taxation, public ownership and expanded public services. Since this was the direction in which policies were moving, Labor was seen as the party of initiative (in the original phrasing by W.K. Hancock, the "party of movement"). By contrast, while the Liberals went with the general flow, they were the party of resistance, seeking to slow change and protect the interests of their own base in lower taxation and small government.

Since neither party could command a reliable majority, it was necessary to campaign on policies that attracted swinging voters. This encouraged convergence to the political centre but not enough to obscure the differences between the parties.

The economic chaos of the 1970s reversed the steady flow towards the left that had characterised politics since Federation. The Hawke–Keating government adopted, willingly or otherwise, the policy package then called "economic rationalism" and now generally described as "neoliberalism." However, policies like Medicare and the Accord with the trade unions produced a "soft" version of neoliberalism, contrasting with the hard neoliberalism of Thatcher in the UK and Howard in Australia.

Labor received 49.5 per cent of the primary vote in 1983, but this achievement would never be repeated. Labor voters drifted off, first to the Australian Democrats and then to the Greens. At the same time, the economic and social changes associated with economic rationalism eroded Labor's traditional base to the point of insignificance. In the 1960s, most workers were in blue-collar jobs, and the great majority were union members (not always willingly). Labor could win elections simply by securing solid support from this group, particularly on the (then standard) assumption that wives would vote like their husbands. In practice, however, conservative parties gained enough working-class support to remain electorally dominant.

The shift to a service economy, along with legislation abolishing "closed shops" and conversion of employees to notionally independent contractors, has changed the picture radically. The three biggest blue-collar unions (the CFMEU, AMWU and AWU) have about 200,000 members between them, barely more than 1 per cent of the electorate. The entire group of wage workers in trades and labouring occupations accounts for a little under 20 per cent of the workforce and perhaps 13 per cent of the electorate, not all of whom vote Labor. The group commonly identified as Labor's "base" amounts to about 10 per cent of voters.

Given that Labor currently secures about 35 per cent of first-preference votes, what drives the decisions of the 25 per cent of the population who don't fit the "base" model?

First, there is a group with a "football team" identification with Labor, perhaps inherited from their parents. Albanese himself fits this model, almost to the point of caricature. Kelly's reference to Albanese's "three great faiths – Labor, the Rabbitohs and the Catholic Church" – is central here. Albanese's identification with the Catholic Church does not imply belief in its doctrines, any more than his support for the Rabbitohs during their forty years in the rugby league wilderness reflected admiration of their playing strategies. In both cases, the strongest passion is that of not being on the other side: that of the Anglican establishment or the (silvertail) Sydney Roosters. As Kelly astutely observes, "Above all else, [Albanese] is *not* a Liberal," even if his policies consist mainly of marginal adjustments to the settings he inherited after nine years of Liberal government.

Closely related to this kind of identification is an uncritical acceptance of the two-party system. Lots of voters don't fully understand preferential voting (indeed, until very recently, lots of political journalists didn't) and assume that a vote for Labor is the most effective way of expressing a preference for a Labor, rather than LNP, government. Many are misled by phrases such as "hung parliament," implying, contrary to actual experience, that a minority government is likely to be unstable and ineffective.

Finally, there is a segment of the electorate who are, like the idealised swinging voters of the past, voting Labor because they prefer Labor's policy offering, pitched marginally to the left of the Morrison-era LNP, to that of any alternative. The most promising positive elements of the 2022 policy package (the Indigenous Voice to Parliament, the National Anti-Corruption Commission and the Housing Australia Future Fund) have been either failures or disappointments. But as the LNP has shifted further into pointless culture war, centrist and centre-right voters have nowhere else to go.

The result is that Albanese has succeeded in his goal of establishing Labor as the natural party of government. Even if some accident hands the Coalition an election win, they will remain the B team, holding office only intermittently until the natural order is restored. And with the Coalition routinely preferencing the Greens last, Labor's left flank is also secure, at least in the House of Representatives.

The price of this success is that Labor is no longer the party of initiative. The idea that a slow and steady first term in government would lay the basis for real change in the second and third is now forgotten, about as relevant as the party's socialist objective (still part of its official constitution).

Coming back to the title of Kelly's essay, the analysis here suggests a simple answer to the question "What does Labor stand for?"

Labor stands for itself. For the moment, that seems to be enough.

John Quiggin

Correspondence

Judith Brett

Sean Kelly's thoughtful essay ponders the tension between idealism and political pragmatism in understanding the current government's apparent reluctance to spend its unprecedented store of political capital. What, he asks, shapes the Labor Party? Historical faith in the working class? Opposition to Tories? A commitment to socialism?

Kelly criticises Albanese's description of himself to Piers Morgan as "a social democrat who believes in markets but believes that the state ... can make a positive difference to people's lives" for its "dreadful blandness." Albanese's belief in markets is, Kelly writes, a way of avoiding the accusation of being a socialist and "of disavowing strong belief." But it is nothing of the sort.

Labor beliefs draw on two distinct strands of ideas: the power of organised labour to combat exploitation and improve the lives of working-class people; and social democracy, which relies on the powers of the state to moderate the outcomes of capitalist markets to increase equality. Decline in union power and shifting understandings of class have weakened the influence of labourist ideas, but social-democratic ideas remain strong. To appeal to them as Albanese does is not, as Kelly suggests, a disavowal of belief in order to avoid the accusation of socialism, but a statement of claim.

Kelly writes as if socialism means the overthrow of markets and capitalism, but this has never been its meaning in the Australian context. The socialist objective Labor adopted in 1921 was a qualified objective, advocating the national ownership of industries only "to the extent necessary to eliminate exploitation and other antisocial features." On the radical fringe were some who argued that all capitalist enterprises were necessarily exploitative because they relied on surplus value extracted from labour, but the majority supported private property and a mixed economy, placing their faith in union action and government regulation to prevent gross exploitation.

Both the Labor and Liberal parties support markets, private property and an active state. The difference is a matter of degree, with Labor having greater faith in state regulation and state provision to solve social problems, such as the inequalities of class, discrimination against women and minorities and environmental degradation. The Liberals reluctantly play catch-up.

What socialism has meant in Australian political debate has not been opposition to capitalism but belief in the creative and ameliorative capacities of the state to reduce inequality and advance the common good. It took on this meaning early, in the late nineteenth century, when colonial liberals like Alfred Deakin abandoned the belief in a classic laissez-faire state which protected property but left the largest possible scope for the exercise of individual freedom. Colonial liberals such as Deakin and Henry Bourne Higgins, who delivered the famous *Harvester* judgment, which laid the foundation for the minimum wage, embraced social liberalism's argument that the state should provide everyone with the opportunity to lead a fulfilling life by, for example, providing free public education, regulating working conditions in shops and factories and resolving industrial disputes. Labor parties, emerging in the 1890s, saw the state as a potential means to advance their aims if they could win office. In 1903, free trade being a lost cause, the leader of the federal Opposition, George Reid, renamed his Free Trade Party the Anti-Socialist Party to signal that it was against government regulation. Robert Menzies attacked Labor's plans for post–World War II Australia as socialist, even as he embraced many of the expansions in the role of government Labor had implemented during the war. By the end of the 1940s both the Labor and Liberal parties shared a commitment to full employment, expanded welfare provision and government-led economic development. Where they differed was over the extent of government planning, regulation and ownership: Labor for more, Liberals for less – and they called Labor's more "socialism."

The postwar consensus on an active, expansive role for government collapsed in the mid-1970s, to be replaced by a new consensus that government regulation and provision needed to be wound back. It was argued that a new balance was needed between government and the market in the distribution of resources to free up the productivity-enhancing powers of competitive markets and return Western economies to growth. The remedies were to reduce government spending, deregulate government-controlled markets, privatise government-owned enterprises and contract out the delivery of government-funded services. This was neoliberalism, first called economic rationalism in Australia, and again the difference between the parties was a question of balance and degree. The Coalition wanted faster and more comprehensive deregulation of the labour market in particular and the curbing of union power. And it wanted faster privatisation of Australia's monopoly telecommunications provider, Telecom. Labor, on the other hand, paired its support for market mechanisms in determining the distribution of resources with a strengthening of what it called the "social wage."

The centrepiece of this was Medicare, a new national health scheme, which the Coalition opposed all the way, as it had the version introduced by the Whitlam government as Medibank. It was not until 1995 that John Howard in his second stint as Liberal leader abandoned the Coalition's opposition. This was not because of conviction. Electoral pragmatism forced him to play catch-up. By then Medicare was bedded down and a clear electoral asset for Labor on the side of government action, as it has continued to be. Hence the symbolic power of Albanese waving his green Medicare card during the election campaign. It was a powerful statement of belief that the power of the state can make a positive difference in people's lives.

Judith Brett

THE GOOD FIGHT

Correspondence

Alison Pennington

With the elevation of the Hawke–Keating period within federal Labor's ranks, you may have missed that Anthony Albanese reserved his more inspired rhetoric for Labor's wartime and reconstruction leaders, Curtin and Chifley. In the middle of US tariff war negotiations, the PM's Curtin Oration in 2025 laid out the former leader's legacy in charting Australia's foreign policy on our own terms, while at the UK Labour conference Albanese celebrated Atlee and Chifley as leaders who worked "to build societies worthy of those who'd fought to defend the world from fascism and tyranny."

What does it mean that Albanese is yet to integrate the nation-building reforming spirit of his wartime inspirations into domestic politics, presently reserved for Bob Hawke's consensus model? With neoliberal globalism collapsing and an erratic global US hegemon threatening world war, the pursuit of sovereign reconstruction and new alliances which delivered decades of security and prosperity for post-war Australia would seem a better fit in our times. Certainly the "Trump factor" behind Labor's thumping electoral victory in 2025 demonstrates the people's appetite.

Behind Albanese's global/domestic taxonomy of former Labor leaders is an inner struggle to break with the crisis-ridden neoliberal model generating economic ruin and political reaction across the world – a model birthed by Labor's own heroes in Hawke and Keating. By "breaking the model," I mean constructing a new way of doing government that resolves established failures of privatisation, monopoly, outsourcing layered on outsourcing (for example, the National Disability Insurance Scheme, the National Broadband Network), low private investment, regulation, short-term budgeting, individualised workplace relations and the decline of shared civic life. This is no small feat.

Contest and conflict between different economic interests has been airbrushed out of Australian politics. For decades, people have been told that growth, higher profits, better government services and rising living standards were all possible, all at once. But with inequality exploding, an outdated tax system making it worse, and Australia's social compact with wage earners unravelling due to housing unaffordability, it's impossible for Albanese's Labor to continue claiming these are still mutually reinforcing goals. But with the exception of IR reforms in the first term of government, the consensus politics of the Hawke model prevails, through gritted-teeth smiles.

Unlike in the fortunate epoch of Hawke and Keating, the days of having one's cake and eating it too are over. As Kelly's essay makes clear, Albanese's Labor is yet to articulate what it stands for. Is it attempting a social-democratic or democratic-socialist program, per the party's constitution? That is, is it seeking to incrementally reroute social relations away from the profit motive towards non-profit, state or community control? Or is it continuing along the path of Australian neoliberalism?

The protracted crisis in government-funded services is the pointy end of this question. Since the 1980s, the party has relied on handing big public spends to private actors to sell the idea of welfare state expansion, and to avoid any confrontation with business interests. But a simple reliance on so-called "markets" to deliver reforms everywhere – including the NDIS, childcare, aged care and housing – isn't possible, as outsourcing undermines provision itself. Nowhere is this more evident than in childcare, where systemic criminal abuse of infants adds to the litany of outsourcing failures, representing a major problem for Albanese, who wants universal childcare to be his defining legacy.

In *The Age of Uncertainty*, John Kenneth Galbraith says the Anglo-American leadership instinct, where citizens look to politicians in high office to solve big problems, is "not the politics of people but the politics of leaders." He reminds us that this isn't universal, with many people and cultures looking to the collective responsibility and intelligence of the people when solving problems. I think much of Sean Kelly's reflection boils down to this central question: can we justifiably blame Albanese and federal Labor for a lack of leadership or structural reform, or do we point to wider social malaise, immobilisation and other structural factors dragging on leadership everywhere? Is it the leader, or the lack of an active citizenry directing or signalling to the leadership?

I see plenty of effort within Albanese Labor to plot a new direction. But they reach roadblocks and lack the firepower to push through, oscillating between optimism for social-democratic revival and cynical resignation that we cannot really buck global capitalist forces, only ride them out in "the Australian way" (that is, the "Third Way," pioneered by Hawke and the inspiration for Blairism). What stops half-measures from becoming full measures? I think there are some key explanations for the blockages.

First, Australia is unique among Anglophone countries for the historical influence of wider civil society organisations, especially unions, on the foundations and functioning of our democracy. That is, Australia's leadership model was conceived with a strong dose of horizontal, citizen-led problem-solving. Formed in the 1890s, the ALP is a creation of unionised workers who wanted to spread their considerable workplace power into a democratic state. Pledges were imposed by unions on their representatives that they would commit to what they were put into parliament to achieve. This pledge culminated in the socialist objective, the "democratic socialisation of industry, production, distribution and exchange," which is still in the ALP's national constitution, with a wriggle-room caveat added later: "to the extent necessary to eliminate exploitation and other anti-social features."

By reaching into workplaces, unions brought everyday people's perspectives, hopes, dreams and demands into parliament. They were authorities on "how to be a human being," and by listening to them Labor had confidence it was walking with the people. No governing through polling needed.

The centrality of strong unions to the origin story of our democracy is the reason why industrial relations is still the unifying ground for *both* the ALP and the Coalition. In the 1940s, the Liberal Party formed because of concern about the rising power of unions and the ALP in society. Coalition with the Nationals was based on fortifying opposition to unions while using government power to embolden business. Sussan Ley's recent desperation to repair net-zero party fractures by returning to IR shows yet again that curtailing unions is always fertile, unifying ground for conservatives.

Recall that Bob Hawke was elected off the back of this once-vibrant democratic infrastructure, with 55 per cent of workers members of their union when he took office. Big reforms were tackled by harnessing unions – most notably, in the Accords – with positions arrived at through fierce debate and negotiation, and with a governing tool available to reliably reach the working population and most of the business sector.

The fact is there is no such wave for Albanese to ride. In part, because the Accords demobilised unions, and the decades of technocratic super-union reform and labour market deregulation that followed have severely reduced union influence. Labor could go further than the first-term IR reforms to lift unionisation, unleashing a democratic revival through measures that incentivise membership, including ending free-riding. But that would require Albanese to kill the cultivated "consensus" image he learnt at the feet of Hawke.

The declining health of unions has an outsized impact on the health and operation of the ALP, more than on any comparable party in the world. Kelly points out that Albanese is clear on what Labor is not – a Liberal, a conservative or "purist" Green – but isn't clear on what Labor stands for. Here is the real crisis for the two-party dynamic. The loss of union power and the capacity for cooperative effort everywhere is a crisis of purpose and representation for both parties. In reality, the ALP is still learning how to operate without an organised working class.

Asserting leadership amid a historic decline in social organisation was already a task, but the Albanese government must also contend with the rise of a new US-cultivated, anti-establishment right intent on dismantling the redistributive welfare state, liberalism and the international rules-based order. It is a mood spreading through all of Australia's Western allies in the United States, Europe, UK and New Zealand. As Trump moves on from the neoliberal consensus into something darker and older, the space for Albanese's Labor to entertain the status quo or push for any incremental social-democratic possibility is being actively undermined – or closed off.

This is no small adjustment for Australia, as a small, trade-exposed country located very far from its closest ally. It is fast-tracking questions about our relationship to China and how to best protect our interests. It is brand-new territory for the government, and a big driver of caution and tiptoeing. The terrain for decision-making is like quicksand.

Political discourse often conflates politicians or parliament with "government" as a totality, as though elected leaders were inclusive of all the nuts and bolts of actual governing. But it is the tangible resources available to elected representatives that determine their success, and this includes a strong and capable public administration to enact the democratic will.

As Kelly says, "passive language … makes you passive," and a force for overwhelming passivity and ceiling-setting is the state of the federal public service. It is impossible to overstate the challenge Albanese's Labor faces here. When I was a senior staffer, I found the biggest challenge of my job, as for many staffers, was working out how to squeeze reform out of a sclerotic APS lacking in confidence and capacity. It was working out how to translate ministerial ambition and direction into tangibles.

Albanese Labor holds to the principle of rebuilding a "frank and fearless" federal administration – after decades of deskilling, outsourcing and funding cuts. But the reality of rebuilding public service leadership from a very low point means that asserting direction, or having confidence that things will be done, is not a straightforward process. Sometimes the only option is very patient collaboration, and large amounts of hand-holding. Like geopolitical repositioning, the road to rebuilding the government's capacity to do stuff is slow and painful.

Now the Albanese government has the tough task of attempting reform in the absence of strong signals from an active, organised citizenry that would create the political space for it to act. Harder still, it must reform top-down alongside a generation of public servants without any experience of delivering federal reforms, government services or building stuff. This is risky business. The big question we should ask is: should we ever seek major reform in the absence of constituencies' capacity to demand and implement it? Incrementalism feels inevitable.

Yet incrementalism is less and less possible for Albanese. Australia's economic conditions are already closing the space for slow social-democratic reform, which depends as a strategy on both a growing economy and a reliable, predictable flow of the benefits of that growth to everyday people. Australia may have escaped the stagnation and reduced living standards that hit Europe and the United States after the global financial crisis, but since the pandemic inflation crisis we have firmly entered a new period, with rising inequality, slowing productivity growth and a persistent threat of inflation.

While the Albanese government was protecting us from supposedly "imported international events" such as the Russia–Ukraine conflict, it delayed the hard work of confronting our homegrown problems, including big untaxed wealth, monopolies, and an investor-dominated housing system. Now the domestic is coming to bite it on the bum. Our conditions demand a confrontation with the conflicts inherent in the economy between the haves and the have-nots. Albanese Labor must accept that this is a period of inevitable conflict, choose a side and take up the fight.

Galbraith defined the essence of leadership as "the willingness to confront unequivocally the major anxiety of their people in their time." In 2026, Albanese Labor faces choices about how to respond to that rising anxiety. Australia could be an internationally celebrated case of how to be brave when you're small, delinking from an illiberal United States and finding new friends. We could avoid the rightward drift by doing what other Western countries have failed to do, by rethinking and reinventing how a social-democratic state delivers public goods and economic and social equality in new times, actions that mirror those taken by the Prime Minister's inspirations in Curtin and Chifley.

Albanese Labor needs clear-eyed, ambitious and definitive breaks with current practice. It's not an easy route, but our own post-war history proves it's possible both to build an ambitious project of mass prosperity and to shield Australia from a dangerous empire in decline so that we may engage with the world on our own terms.

Alison Pennington

Luara Ferracioli

In his compelling and philosophically rich Quarterly Essay, Sean Kelly addresses several questions that many voters must have asked themselves since Labor took office. What do Prime Minister Anthony Albanese and his Labor government stand for? How different is Labor from the Opposition? What are we, the citizenry, entitled to expect from Labor in its second term?

Kelly entertains many generous answers to these questions but finishes the essay with a provocative suggestion: Labor is now best characterised as an essentially conservative party in charge of a conservative government. Labor has become so preoccupied with policies that are compatible with the interests of the vast majority of citizens that it simply cannot deliver for the most vulnerable segments of the population, those who have the most to gain from serious socioeconomic reforms.

To support his suggestion, Kelly argues that all the redistributive policies that would be required to truly realise social justice in Australia have been treated as taboo since Albanese took office: inheritance tax, reduced funding for private schools, getting rid of the profit motive in childcare, aged care and disability care, reforming capital gains tax, and limiting or abolishing negative gearing and superannuation tax concessions.

Kelly argues that because Labor wants to govern for the majority of citizens, who benefit from the existing arrangements, it makes sense to aim at simply maintaining the status quo, tinkering at the edges. Kelly's contention is that to stay in power and become the natural party of government in Australia, Labor has decided to abandon its progressive commitments, merely making things slightly better for vulnerable Australians.

Although I think Kelly is right to question Labor's motives in explaining its inability to bring about significant socioeconomic reform since the 2022 election, I think he is wrong to suggest that Labor has lost sight of its progressive values.

Labor is still progressive at heart. The problem is that it does not seem to fully understand the temporal dimension of the challenges facing Australia. It also seems unable to recognise that political leadership is sometimes about moral leadership.

Before I defend Labor's progressive credentials, I want to explore Kelly's suggestion a bit further. Why should we think Labor is now a conservative party? One potential explanation for this conservatism is that Labor has, in effect, become the *liberal* party of Australia. The idea here is that while the Coalition has become distracted by unproductive culture wars, Labor has become the party focused on creating the conditions for all citizens to pursue the good by their own lights, with the government interfering only to maintain the rule of law and to provide the citizenry with a safety net, ensuring that "no one is left behind."

There is something to this explanation, and in fact I think a commitment to these liberal values played an important role in their electoral success in 2025. While the Greens were taking sides in the gender wars, the Liberals in the multicultural wars, and the Nationals in the climate wars, the public saw Labor as a party that seemed genuinely interested in governing for all Australians, determined to find consensus on difficult and controversial matters.

But simply because Labor has become more committed to individual freedom and consensus, it is a mistake to think it has abandoned its egalitarian aspirations. For one thing, liberalism and egalitarianism are not only compatible but mutually reinforcing. For another, one finds many appeals to egalitarianism in Albanese's speeches. During his first victory speech, he said: "I hope there are families in public housing watching this tonight. Because I want every parent to be able to tell their child no matter where you live or where you come from, in Australia the doors of opportunity are open to us all. And like every other Labor government, we'll just widen that door a bit more." More recently, he has stated: "You constantly progress and move forward … To a more inclusive society. To one that has greater opportunity regardless of people's birth or people's ethnicity or religion or gender."

The philosophical commitment behind these comments is clear: a child growing up in public housing should be just as likely as a child growing up in a harbourside mansion to occupy positions of power and influence and to lead a life they value. A child's family wealth (or lack thereof) should not be allowed to dictate how their life goes. This is a deeply egalitarian sentiment.

I am not disputing that Labor is *behaving* like a conservative government. That is certainly how it looks from the outside. Rather, I am claiming that we still find a commitment to egalitarian values in Labor. True conservatives are not in the business of aspiring towards a more inclusive society, for realising this kind of aspiration requires significant changes to existing institutions and social practices.

So perhaps the explanation here is about risk. Perhaps Albanese still sees himself as progressive but believes the risk of trying to implement egalitarian policies is too high. The diagnosis of Labor's complacency is that, although it wants to do more, it does not want to risk the return of the Coalition to power.

This explanation is equally unconvincing. Surely Albanese knows that the conditions have never been more favourable for serious egalitarian reform in Australia and that no government will never face a more ineffective and confused Opposition. In fact, there is currently no serious alternative government in Australia. In addition to losing a significant number of seats in the previous election, the Opposition has become considerably divided. Classical liberals are split between the Liberal Party and the teals. Conservatives are divided between the Liberal Party, One Nation and the Nationals. At the moment, the closest we get to a unified Opposition in Australia is the Greens, but they are the party most likely to welcome egalitarian reforms. There has never been a better time, as far as lack of effective Opposition is concerned, to bring about egalitarian policies in Australia, and Albanese knows this. We all know this.

Here is the best explanation of the lack of progress on Labor's part: Labor believes that going slowly is the *only* way to get the public on board with the changes needed to create a more egalitarian society. The ideals are liberal-egalitarian, but Albanese thinks Australians will only accept widening the doors of opportunity if the government pushes them open slowly.

Kelly concedes that this is a big part of the story but seems to think that this attitude inevitably commits Labor to a form of conservatism. I think this attitude can also be explained by a fundamental misunderstanding on the part of Labor of the unfairness at the heart of our current institutional and policy settings.

Indeed, the main challenge we face as Australians is intergenerational inequality and going slowly simply makes the problem worse. Every year that children receive unequal levels of education, the harder it is for them to compete fairly for tertiary education and well-paid jobs in adulthood. Every year a young person can't afford to go to university, the harder it will be for them ever to get a degree. Every year that a middle-aged adult rents, the less able they are to afford or pay off a mortgage before retirement.

In many cases, a failure to act now means the doors of opportunity will be closed forever. This is clearest in the case of family-making. Many Australians are choosing not to have a family because it is prohibitively expensive. A government that chooses to move slowly towards making child-rearing less expensive will not be in a position to compensate these individuals for this lost opportunity later. After all, those who missed out on parenthood in early to mid-adulthood do not typically get to become parents later in life. Put simply, not all lost opportunities can be compensated for at a later date.

Every year of inaction makes Australia more intergenerationally unequal. This means that the problem gets worse and becomes much harder to fix. Every year of going slowly robs each generation of the meaningful opportunities that previous generation enjoyed. This is fundamentally unfair.

So, the option of going slowly is both risky and unfair. It risks making the problem worse, and it treats young people unfairly by expecting them to wait for changes they might never benefit from. It also fails to take seriously the fact that every citizen is only a child once, a young person once, a young adult once, and that each life stage requires access to experiences that are valuable in themselves but also that set one up to lead a better life in the future.

According to Kelly, Treasurer Jim Chalmers' theory is that "people will cop big things done slowly and little things done quickly, but not big things done quickly or little things done slowly." Is this right? Only if one takes societal attitudes for granted, which is odd since societal attitudes are themselves a result of moral leadership on the part of political leaders. What the people believe in, desire and care about can be shaped by the ideas discussed and advocated for in the public arena by our political leaders. They can be shaped, in particular, by the story the government prosecutes on behalf of those who have been or will be treated unfairly if difficult decisions are not made. In other words, going slowly is one option. Telling a compelling moral story about ourselves and about what it means to truly realise the fair go in Australia is another.

The way the public responded to the change to the stage-three tax cuts is the best illustration of this point. Of course, a lot of people were going to be disappointed. But the government made a compelling case for the change, and it was handsomely rewarded at the last election.

A similar dynamic took place during the pandemic. Prime Minister Scott Morrison (and state premiers) got the citizenry to make huge sacrifices in their basic liberties for the benefit of vulnerable members of society. The narrative that justified those sacrifices appealed to an ideal of what type of society we wanted to be: one that protects its elderly citizens from a serious virus. The changes were not made slowly. If anything, radical changes were made on an almost daily basis. But the government provided the necessary moral leadership by reminding Australians that we value the lives of the elderly as much as we value the lives of the young.

Albanese can tell a similar story that reminds well-off older citizens that young citizens deserve meaningful opportunities to flourish, and that younger citizens will lose hope in their future, and in the future of this country, unless we act swiftly to stop the intergenerational gap from widening. If children from working-class backgrounds leave school not as well equipped for the jobs of the future as children attending elite private schools, or if young people choose not to go to university or not to study something they are passionate about because they cannot afford it, we deny many members of a generation the ability to achieve the life they value. The same is true if young people can't afford a house where their family, communities and jobs are, or if they cannot afford to have children.

We all lose in a world where young people don't reach their potential. We lose in productivity, ingenuity, creativity. We make Australia worse for everyone even if some of us are better off in a narrow sense because we are paying less tax than we would under a more egalitarian tax setting.

Labor is the liberal egalitarian party of Australia. It has a strategy, but mistakenly thinks it can only bring about egalitarian reform by slow change.

But when it comes to intergenerational inequality, this strategy only makes the problem worse and robs young people of opportunities they are entitled to as a matter of social justice. Labor must speed up, or the good fight will have been lost before it has properly begun.

Luara Ferracioli

Correspondence

Ankit Kumar

There is a cliché that two types of people work in Parliament House: wonks and hacks. The wonks are idealists who see politicians as vehicles of policy change for the country. The hacks are fighters who enjoy the combat of winning debates, getting power and surviving in the media jungle.

Sean Kelly was unusual: as a press secretary, he cared about winning the day's news, but also about fighting the good fight. While I served as Kevin Rudd's Health Policy Adviser, Sean was my dependable, thoughtful partner for years, first as Press Secretary to the Health Minister (Nicola Roxon) and then for prime ministers Rudd and Gillard. We spent many months travelling with Rudd as he struggled to make health reform Labor's signature issue.

One memory from those days still haunts me. On 27 April 2010, while the prime minister was visiting Nepean Hospital, the media got wind that the government was dropping emissions trading, which the PM had previously said was the "greatest moral challenge of our time." Sean had the abysmal task of talking Rudd through the suggested lines: that it had been "delayed" due to Senate opposition and slow global commitments. He did it with incredible grace. The disappointment of that day, and similar moments during government, echo in the mood of his insightful essay.

In this piece, Sean sheds his cloak as a former Labor insider to find his active voice. He rightly notes that our economic frameworks and the structures they have spawned are tending towards a more unequal and fragile society. Meanwhile, centre-left politics in Australia (and globally) is seeking a rallying vision. Though Sean doesn't dwell on it, his message feels all the more urgent against the muscularity of the right. His picture of the philosophical and pragmatic dilemmas centre-left parties face should be compulsory reading for political staffers globally.

Yet in his charge of "gradualism," I can't help but think he is asking too much of the Albanese Labor government. In London, where I'm writing from and where

Keir Starmer stormed into power in 2024, UK Labour *dreams* of being as united, confident and re-electable as its Australian namesake. Like Albanese, Starmer won almost two-thirds of the parliamentary seats with one of the lowest primary votes in a long time, also a "wide and shallow" win. But then Starmer, like Albanese, had to govern. Starmer tried cutting the winter fuel subsidy and curbing steep rises in disability payouts. The party got him to back down. He floated taxing private equity and the City of London got him to drop it. Instead, he taxed large estate holders but then carved out farms. Most major policies have been followed by a backdown. The sum of these failures has robbed UK Labour of the funds needed to offset their election promises to reduce child poverty, like scrapping the two-child benefit cap. So it has fallen back on raising wage levies faced by employers, forcing a showdown with pubs and restaurants, and breathing life into the Tories' charge that Labour only knows "tax and spend."

To be fair, the United Kingdom is in more of a mess. Government debt is more than double Australia's as a share of the economy. One in every £10 of government spending goes to interest payments. The UK has an older population, slower growth, and a major war a short flight away. Starmer faced a bunch of bad choices. But Starmer's paralysis should remind us that while Albanese's ambition will not please the purists, holding one's party together and consolidating popularity deserves respect. When your opponents outside and within the party have seen the blood in the water, they know they can always come back. In January 2026, *The Guardian* editorialised on the damage to Labour's ability to govern in this way: "the combination of combative stances and capitulation has many debilitating effects. It makes the prime minister look weak. It is a disincentive to loyalty, because ministers who dare defend unpopular positions in public soon discover they were wasting their time."

Sean is right in arguing that the Albanese government is best understood in light of the Rudd/Gillard years. That was Australian Labor's big bang moment, where eleven years of frustrated progressive ambition spawned a nonstop series of mega-announcements: taking on mining companies, polluters, state governments, private health insurance, Telstra, big tobacco – the list goes on. The running line in the Prime Minister's Office was that if it wasn't the first in the world or the biggest in Australian history, it wouldn't get Rudd's attention. The government was stretched across so many fronts there wasn't enough time or capacity to see policies through.

If you see Labor as a multigenerational project, there is a role for governments like Albanese's. The National Disability Insurance Scheme, Paid Parental Leave, the National Broadband Network, the Gonski reforms and even simply entrenching the legitimacy of the Fair Pay Commission is necessary work for the Labor movement. Sean concedes that the social media ban may yet be seen as a defining policy. Certainly, the speed with which copycat proposals are sprouting on both sides of politics across rich countries signals it has created a new paradigm.

Watching from overseas, you can't help but feel that Albanese is doing something right. When I speak to Labor colleagues back home, there is the ghostly familiarity of speaking with Democrats during Obama's second term. There's a sense that hope is waning, disillusionment has set in, and dreams are fading as the window gets smaller. They want to go back to the old guys – Obama the orator and Albanese the street fighter. Yet I suspect that once they find themselves deep in the dystopia of a Trump or Farage, they will look back affectionately to when Labor ran the country with caution and dignity, and without graft.

There is one other formative professional experience that Sean doesn't dwell on. From 2007 to 2013, Albanese was Leader of Government Business (and from 2006 to 2007 Manager of Opposition Business). He was responsible for organising parliamentary tactics and making sure that Labor "won" the optics of televised question time every single day. Sean was in the room with Albanese, Rudd, Gillard, Wong, Faulkner and top media staff as they plotted the lines and attacks against the Opposition. Albanese was a force in those meetings. No one would doubt that was his forum. He is the master parliamentary tactician of his generation. Today he runs a government the way he used to run tactics: playing it a day at a time, obsessing over the optics of holding course, steering a little to the left or right, or changing the topic.

It is easy to dismiss this true talent of Anthony Albanese, to relegate it to "politics." But politics at this moment is exceptionally difficult, chaotic and destabilising. Albanese has manoeuvred his party to a place where the trajectories of Australian Labor and UK Labour are wildly different. The former is positioned to achieve complex reforms over a long period and, as Sean tells us, paint Australian Labor as the natural party of government. While UK Labour lacerates itself and struggles to take a forward step, Australian Labor may navigate this age of chaos and exhaustion and could become the sort of government that Sean wants.

Ankit Kumar

Chris Tallentire

My former colleagues in the Western Australian Parliamentary Labor Party are good and honourable people, determined to do the best for those they represent. But sometimes, on some vital issues, something goes wrong and the wishes of vested interests prevail. Then, like Sean Kelly in *The Good Fight*, one is left wondering: what does Labor stand for?

Labor defines itself by not being its opponent, says Kelly, making the case that there's a shift to a new opponent. He says the old internal battles of idealism versus pragmatism, where accommodations had to be made, have given way to an opposition to the external "purity" now owned by the Greens.

The massive state election win in March 2021 saw WA Labor win fifty-three of fifty-nine seats in the Legislative Assembly. The WA government's management of the Covid-19 pandemic had been outstanding – WA Labor stood for competence – and voters were minded to reward Premier Mark McGowan and his team. The pandemic had provided a once-in-a-lifetime window into what a Labor government can do. The bond of confidence between voters and decision-makers was extraordinary, so voters returned us to office to make real and lasting change.

What would WA Labor politicians do in this precious new era? How could we nurture and maintain the bond of confidence? What could we do that a Coalition government would never do? How could we deliver for ordinary working people now and for future generations? How could we secure our extraordinary natural environment for future generations? How could we adapt to our fast-changing climate?

To their credit, former premier McGowan and current premier Roger Cook embrace the idea of governing for all and making WA Labor the natural party of government. Politicians are notorious for wanting to please everyone, but there's a time when choices must be made. From ancient Greek philosophy, this is the time for *phronesis* – the essence of politics. The time when a government must determine its priorities for improving the lives of people while assessing what's politically feasible.

We had done the hard work and now found ourselves in an extraordinary position to debate and discuss reforms for which we had all been calling for decades. In this new political reality, no progressive policy was off-limits. This was a unique opportunity to shape and modernise WA legislation to provide safety, security and equality for all West Australians.

This could have been small acts, such as removing the daily recital of the non-secular Lord's Prayer from the Parliament. It could have been as ambitious as ramping up funding for public housing so that no West Australian child would be forced to couch-surf or live in a car. It could be modernising Western Australia's *Equal Opportunity Act* to ensure staff and children in schools funded under the WA *Education Act* could not be discriminated against for their beliefs, gender or sexuality. It could have been modernising piecemeal and outdated water legislation to help us better cope with a rapidly drying climate. It could have been funding endangered species recovery plans, providing real pathways to prevent extinction.

When the last WA Labor government came to power in 2001 with Geoff Gallop as premier, it came into government unafraid to engage with people. The Gallop government's approach emphasised a partnership between government, industry and the community, resulting in Western Australia becoming a leader at a national level in the absence of a national climate policy framework. The state water strategy drove important efficiency measures across households and government; desalinisation plants were built as the science showed that the southwest of Western Australia was one of the world's regions most severely affected by declining annual rainfall and reduced run-off into dams.

What many progressive voters have come to realise with shock and dismay is that the WA Labor government of the 2020s does not reach out to the community for ideas or input. Nor does it seek input from its own MPs, who are tightly managed and lectured on staying in their own lane, leaving all decision-making to an inner circle of cabinet members and ministerial advisers.

In a discussion about vested interests and public policy reform, Emeritus Professor Ross Garnaut AC was asked about the difference between the Hawke–Keating government and current Labor governments. Garnaut said the people advising ministers tend to be much more sensitive to perceptions of the immediate political pluses and minuses and that this reacting to the political moment inhibits capturing the enthusiasm of the broader electorate for substantial change.

The power of vested interests to get WA Labor to adopt their policy positions is alarming. The steady stream of cosy business-sector breakfasts and lunches where the premier or a senior minister talks tough about cutting red tape and helping business – especially big corporates – shows the trap WA Labor has fallen into. While it's hard for lay and elected party members to advance their policy ideas, there's an easy willingness to accept policy ideas from vested interests.

This happened in the last parliament with a push by industry peak bodies to weaken Western Australia's environmental protection laws, while simultaneously undermining then federal environment minister Tanya Plibersek's Nature Positive reforms. A review process was contrived, without input from environmental organisations, that gifted industry environmental law reforms which removed an appeal right and enabled the Environmental Protection Authority to include industry people in its membership.

Even more worrying has been WA Labor's treatment of climate-change legislation. This was a 2021 election promise. Far from being a bill about one of the biggest threats to the state and wanting people to come on the journey with them, the general public was excluded from consultation and only targeted stakeholders were consulted over a brief four-week period.

When questions were asked by WA Labor MPs for further evidence supporting the WA government's reiteration of fossil-fuel company Woodside's mantra that WA's export gas was decarbonising Asia, the government decided to pull the entire bill. This was pure pandering to the wishes of vested interests. When faced with the choice between a bill that met the standard set by the federal government, with its legislated independent Climate Change Authority and going to an election with no climate legislation, a situation which suited the gas industry, WA Labor chose the latter.

What does WA Labor stand for? There's a real risk that WA Labor powerbrokers have created a monster, promoting the view that only through absolute discipline can electoral success be continued. This is wrong; the electorate expects us to be dealing with the most pressing questions of our time, as we did during the Covid pandemic. Dismissing reasoned argument as ideological purity and relying on the backing of vested interest groups is bad politics. It's a far cry from what Labor really should stand for. But there's something bigger at stake here, which applies to everyone reading this: the fact that institutions like the Australian Labor Party are shaped by us. It's our responsibility to be involved, arguing the case, knowing that collective action can make a difference. Whatever our capability and contribution, we can all help improve the lives of everyone, tackling the major issues of our time and helping the vulnerable. Ultimately, the question is: what do we stand for?

Chris Tallentire

Georgina Woods

I was intrigued to read in Sean Kelly's excellent essay that a journalist asked Anthony Albanese what end progressives believe Australia is progressing towards. The Prime Minister's answer is illuminating: "Well, there is no endpoint, by definition." Progress was the core belief uniting mainstream political parties in Australia, made possible by growth. Its end seemed unimaginable, but growth needs death, mulch and upheaval.

A recent review by Florence Sutcliffe-Braithwaite in *The London Review of Books* about a new history of Liverpool (the English one) since World War II cited remarks by "Battling Bessie" Braddock, who served the community as an MP, trade unionist and valiant progressive reformer. About drowning a Welsh village under a dam to supply Liverpool with water for industry in the mid-1960s she reportedly said, "Everyone deplores that in the interests of progress, sometimes people must suffer." As it turned out, industry departed from Liverpool not long after that dam was built. In the gamble of modernity, wins are provisional and losses irrevocable.

Losing bargains have been a feature of modernity's ideologies since its inception, whatever their other differences. It is this bargain that puts dust in kids' lungs in the Hunter Valley and lead in their blood in Mount Isa. It drives wildlife to extinction and saps rivers of their lifeblood. The boon of the bargain is modernity's promise: we will industrialise your landscape, uproot your community, demolish your history, but you will have "the good life" – a living, education and health, leisure and all the mod cons.

Progress demands growth. It doesn't stop with one dam, or one mine. *There is no endpoint, by definition.* That is the trouble bedevilling the Australian Labor Party. The ethos of modernity says someone must suffer for progress: politics is the practice of how to decide who suffers, and under what conditions. Kelly writes of postponed conflicts. The deep buried conflict is that in order to live the way of middle-class Australia, we pushed that suffering far out of sight, out to the ends of long chains of global capital. What do I know of the toxic factories where plastics I touch every day are made and villagers perish of cancer? Or mines in remote China where material is stripped from the earth that makes my phone glow, or the upper atmosphere where the pollutants I create will make hell for our descendants? These are the wages of the "good life" of modernity.

As I write this, I feel defences being thrown up by my compatriots reading it: these are not conflicts for which we want to feel responsible. The truth of our lives and the experience of our lives are so divergent that we struggle to make coherent sense of any of it.

Modernity cannot deliver its promises, because those promises were made in breach of a functional, reciprocal relationship with the natural systems of the planet. The Labor Party's paralysis is an expression of this problem, because it has, with sincerity, made a bunch of commitments it is increasingly impossible to reconcile. I don't envy its leaders, but they don't serve the country's interests by retreating into denial about it. It is not possible to prevent catastrophic climate change and maintain the "living standards" of over-consumption and waste that have really only become normal in the last half a century. Certainly not if you believe in equality of condition. Now *there's* an unthinkable political belief!

The Labor Party's dilemma gets worse because it must also contend with the chaotic influence of a handful of wealthy people who appear to have neither political convictions nor personal compunction but who understand this dilemma, or intuit it and use it to serve their ends. They have the short-term advantage of not caring about people or the environment, since they mistake wealth and power for independence from society and nature. Such people appeal to the public's own sceptical intuition when the promises of the moderns are doled out again: *this time* you'll work less, get a home, get "the good life," just let us build a bunch of windfarms and data centres and the modernist utopia will be here. Uh-*huh*.

The cynical exploits of these rich nihilists are made possible by the true thing that the Labor Party must face: people no longer believe in the progress myth. They see that the way we live now means our kids will suffer. There is an endpoint and we're living in it. Readers may scoff at last issue's correspondent Glen Gill, who cannot imagine modernity without fossil fuels, but he's not wrong: there's never been a modernity without them. He's also not wrong to query folks who blithely say "decarbonisation" without reckoning with these conflicts.

Kelly sounds gloomy. In answer I have good news or bad news, depending on our imagination. Now that catastrophic climate change is upon us, Australia no longer has the option of not changing. Modernity has unleashed its consequences. Not many people in Australia appreciate what global warming over 1.5°C means for us, but it will be radical change. The meaningful question now is no longer "reform or revolution?" but "What part will you play in the revolution already underway?" Our choice is how we navigate the end of progress, how kind we are. There are radical visions of a different good life – one that can be shared, that is reciprocal, and kind, that gives people the freedom to be themselves, to live! South Americans call it *buen vivir*. It beckons. This good life will be made possible by a wholly different way of conceiving and pursuing politics, and I'm fairly sure left-of-centre political parties won't conceive and pursue it for us.

Georgina Woods

Sean Kelly

The writing of my essay began from a place of uncertainty: what to make of this Labor government? By the time I finished it, I was still uncertain. I had some suspicions, obviously; some instincts. I had grown more convinced that Labor might miss its chance to make significant change; and more concerned about the consequences for the country if it did. I certainly wanted to persuade readers these were genuine possibilities that should be taken seriously. But I knew, too, that my fears might be misplaced.

Unsurprisingly, in the three months since *The Good Fight* was published, I have not suddenly made up my mind one way or another. I remain undecided. Perhaps the Albanese government is doing exactly what it should, exactly what it can, at a strange moment in history. Or perhaps it will change its approach; there are some recent small signs this might be the case. Or perhaps its fate is to become a long-serving placeholder in history: Labor's version of the Fraser government.

And then there is another option, one I mention in the essay: that it is as bold as it sometimes claims to be and we have missed it. In which case it turns out absolutely everybody has missed it. I would encourage anybody interested in the topic to read all of the responses to the essay. Each is original, thoughtful and interesting. Each one adds to my ideas and challenges them.

And yet the most striking fact about them as a group is this: not one tries to make the case that the Albanese Labor government is bold.

In her response, Luara Ferracioli makes a moving argument that damns this lack of boldness. She argues that Labor's decision to go slowly has urgent moral consequences. In the period in which change does not happen, citizens miss out on things that are central to a good life: a happy childhood, a good teacher, university, a good job, having children. "Every citizen is only a child once, a young person once, a young adult once," she writes. They will not get these things back, for the simple reason that none of us gets time back. Over a life, these losses compound.

There are potential political consequences of caution, too – articulated most strongly by Kos Samaras, who argues there has already been a broad "loss of faith in the mechanisms that were supposed to translate economic participation into economic security." If that is not restored, then faith in democracy may fade as well. In case these are not sufficient consequences to shock hardened Labor strategists, Samaras warns too that Labor's voters will leave it. Unhumbly, I quote him: "This is the fate that awaits Labor if Kelly's warning goes unheeded, not defeat at the hands of the Coalition, but slow-motion irrelevance as the party that managed decline while claiming to stand for something more."

There is one clear area of agreement from respondents: that we are in a strange moment. But their conclusions about what that moment requires are split.

Some are in favour of urgency. Georgina Woods reminds us of catastrophic climate change; Tim Dunlop of spreading authoritarianism. These are among the most important problems of our time. Neither Woods nor Dunlop believes Labor has the answers.

Samaras, though, is still hopeful enough to urge Labor to act. He puts forward the practical argument for speed, to sit alongside Ferracioli's moral one: "The question is not whether Labor can slowly dismantle old orthodoxies while maintaining broad appeal. It is whether slow dismantling can outpace the erosion of faith in the political system itself."

But it is also possible to make the opposite case, as two impressive former colleagues of mine, Emma Dawson and Ankit Kumar, show. They argue that these chaotic times are, instead, good reason for Labor to proceed cautiously. That important things can be achieved and are being achieved, slowly – and that going slowly is the wise choice. That the terrain is treacherous and voters are wary.

This is a fair case, made persuasively. And yet, reading it, a thought won't leave me alone: well, how did we get to this chaotic time?

Kumar writes that, speaking to Labor colleagues, "there is the ghostly familiarity of speaking with Democrats during [President Barack] Obama's second term." One day, he writes, when worse times come, Labor people will look back on this time fondly – a time when "Labor ran the country with caution and dignity, and without graft." He is probably right. But my sense is that Trump did not merely come after Obama chronologically. He was in part the consequence of Obama, who failed to challenge the neoliberal orthodoxy with any real heft, a failure symbolised by his decision to bail out the banks in the financial crisis of 2008. Here is Don Watson in Quarterly Essay 95: "There would be no Trump had Obama made American workers his resounding cause, and made the bankers at least seem to pay a price for their rapaciousness."

Doesn't Obama offer Labor a lesson? To put this more simply: most of us would agree the current chaos is in part a result of neoliberal policy and the inequality it has birthed (Dawson in fact makes this point). In which case, shouldn't the Albanese government, at perhaps the same stage of Australian political history as Obama was in American history, take a different path from the one Obama took? Shouldn't it do something significant about those neoliberal policies?

Dawson argues strongly that Labor is already doing a lot, in keeping with its purpose of helping working people. I think she is right. But then I think John Quiggin is also correct when he asserts that Albanese's "policies consist mainly of marginal adjustments to the settings he inherited after nine years of Liberal government."

This is not a contradiction. Labor is doing quite a bit, and those actions shouldn't be dismissed – I refer to quite a few of them in my essay. But are they changing our society? Do they touch the economic structures which shape our lives? To give one example: Dawson points out that real wages are rising and the labour share of the national economy is rising too. I agree these are good things. But are wage rises, in the vast majority of cases, going to be enough to surmount the gap between those who already own assets and those who do not? This is illustrated by the overwhelming number of Australians who no longer believe you can buy a house without parental help.

What these differing responses make clear to me is that there is a significant split in the left. This is sometimes minimised as a small disagreement over speed. In that story, everyone agrees on the broad direction of change, only some people believe that change should happen a little faster than others do.

But this is not really true, or at least does not get at the size of the disagreement. The split is in fact a chasm: between people who broadly believe the system is working – at least sufficiently well that people can, without too many moral qualms from government, be asked to wait – and those who think it is not. Between those who think the system is working sufficiently well to pacify voters for a few more years without threatening the stability of our country and those who think it is not. Between those who think the hard edges can be sanded off to make the system workable and those who have come to believe those hard edges *are* the system.

I want to swerve now, in what I hope is a useful way (we will arrive back at the same place). Judith Brett, one of this nation's greatest political historians, in her expert and analytical response, refers to what she writes is my characterisation of Anthony Albanese's self-description as a social democrat who believes in both markets and the power of the state as bland. But my assertion was subtly but importantly different: that the tendency of much of the left – including Albanese – to proclaim a "belief in markets" is bland. Brett goes on to point out the contribution to Labor's worldview made by social democracy, "which relies on the powers of the state to moderate the outcomes of capitalist markets." Writing about the Australian meaning of "socialism," she refers to "belief in the creative and ameliorative capacities of the state."

Albanese, like all Labor politicians, is free to put this as lucidly as Brett does: with the sense that markets are fine and good but that Labor's focus is on what the state can do, one aspect of which is mitigating markets. But his tone is different: he *believes* in markets. Albanese, it should be noted, has gone further, arguing in 2023 that markets are "a democratic form of expression … If you want to determine what the best chocolate bar is, the market will tell you … Tim Tams are good biscuits because people buy them."

I agree that Labor traditionally, and Albanese now, sees a role for both the state and the private sector. But the shift in emphasis, from mitigating markets to *believing* in them, I think tells us something, especially as it comes at a time when much of the left has begun asking very serious questions about how well markets have served us. There is in fact serious debate about whether markets really operate any longer in a genuine way in most important areas of our lives, with some arguing convincingly that oligopolies have come to mean that capitalism, in its current iteration, has little to do with markets at all.

To say you *believe in markets* seems to operate as a signal. *I am reasonable. I accept the economic orthodoxy.* It is worth noting that since becoming prime minister, Albanese has used the phrase twice: once to conservative commentator Piers Morgan and once at the *Australian Financial Review* business summit. (He also said he believes in "market forces" while speaking to the Nine newspapers; that was when he talked about Tim Tams.)

This *belief in markets* is not a matter of abstract ideology. As Alison Pennington points out, markets have dramatically failed to provide a childcare system free from abuse – and this is undermining the worth of Albanese's ambition to provide universal childcare. Discussion of changing the neoliberal framework is not about revolution. It is, rather, about shifting the assumptions that operate in several of the areas Labor is most focused on, including aged care, childcare and schooling.

This brings me to an important historical question. Some respondents emphasise the continuity in Labor's history. Dawson points out Labor's consistent purpose in helping working people. Brett emphasises the consistency of social-democratic beliefs. Kumar argues that in taking the view of Labor as a "multigenerational project," there is a role for a Labor government that embeds previous Labor reforms (one of the best arguments I have heard for Albanese's approach).

But there are turning points in history too (Brett touches on this). In my essay, I briefly explore the neoliberalism of the Hawke and Keating years. Those governments delivered many good things to this country. It is possible, too, that there was no way to resist the neoliberal tide: that the mitigated version they oversaw was the best possible version. But it is true, too, that much of the move towards the economic framework of our society was put in place during those years. If Labor accepts it must challenge old orthodoxies, this is likely to go hand in hand with a revised reading of its history and a search for new models – if not to supplant Hawke and Keating, at least to run alongside them. Pennington, with recent experience on the inside, notes Albanese's praise of Curtin and Chifley – prime ministers before the neoliberal turn – and urges him to take on their mission of "rethinking and reinventing how a social-democratic state delivers public goods and economic and social equality in new times."

Or there are still more recent Labor experiences to look to, in state government – ones that might provide negative models. Chris Tallentire generously gives us his view of the West Australian Labor government, of which he was recently a part. He evokes the sense of possibility when Labor was re-elected with a huge majority: "We had done the hard work and now found ourselves in an extraordinary position to debate and discuss reforms for which we had all been calling for decades. In this new political reality, no progressive policy was off limits." What could it not do?

As it happened: almost everything.

Tallentire paints a depressing picture of the operation of that government. Some of these elements are mentioned in other responses, too: we could think of them as contemporary characteristics of Labor governments. Too much attention paid to vested interests. The weakened role of unions (and a reluctance to act dramatically to change this). An exaggerated emphasis on the importance of party discipline. Overly centralised power. A lack of belief in the ability to shift the parameters of what is possible through public persuasion.

There is a hopeful note lying, hidden, underneath this list. It is within Labor's power – within a Labor leader's power – to change every item on it.

I noted earlier that the correspondents agreed this was a strange time. I think so too. But it is possible that all of us are wrong: that this is not a special moment, but merely another moment of change and turmoil in an endless series. We think our era is unique, but we are – like most of those before us – wrong. In that case, Albanese Labor will be graded the way most Labor governments are: did it contribute to the improvement of Australian society in ways that are permanent and important?

There is no simple way to go about this task of change. Georgina Woods makes a grim point in relation to modernity and the losses that have always accompanied progress: "politics is the practice of how to decide who suffers, and under what conditions." Labor is in government, so Labor is deciding – right now – who suffers. These are the high moral stakes of governing. There is no shirking them. By the time a government falls, it will have helped some people and failed others; it will have changed people's lives or failed to change them. Almost four years in, Labor MPs should assess who is suffering in our society. Have they done as much as they had hoped to shift this?

That question can't be answered by election victories, which in themselves prove little. As several respondents note, Labor may keep winning for some time yet, almost by default. In political terms, this means that, to crib from John Quiggin, Labor's current approach – whatever you think of it – "seems to be enough."

Is it enough for those within Labor?

Sean Kelly

Judith Brett is emeritus professor of politics at La Trobe University. A former editor of *Meanjin* and columnist for *The Age*, she won the National Biography Award in 2018 for *The Enigmatic Mr Deakin*. She is the author of four Quarterly Essays.

Emma Dawson is executive director of the Chifley Research Centre.

Tim Dunlop writes regularly on Substack. His books include *The New Front Page: New media and the rise of the audience* and *Why the Future Is Workless*.

Luara Ferracioli is an associate professor of philosophy at the University of Sydney.

Sean Kelly is the author of *The Game: A portrait of Scott Morrison*, a columnist for the Nine newspapers and regular contributor to *The Monthly*, and a former adviser to Labor prime ministers.

Ankit Kumar was Senior Policy Adviser for Health to prime ministers Kevin Rudd and Julia Gillard. He has since worked at the OECD and for technology companies in the United Kingdom and United States.

Alison Pennington is Chief Economist of the McKell Institute. She is the author of *Gen F'd: How young Australians can recover their uncertain futures*.

John Quiggin is an Australian Laureate Fellow in economics at the University of Queensland and the author of *Zombie Economics* and *Economics in Two Lessons*. His blog, at johnquiggin.com, presents commentary from a social-democratic viewpoint.

Kos Samaras is director of strategy and analytics at RedBridge and a former Victorian Labor strategist.

Chris Tallentire is a former Labor member of the Western Australian Parliament. Before entering parliament, he was director of the Conservation Council of Western Australia.

Michael Wesley is Professor of Politics and Deputy Vice Chancellor (Global, Culture and Engagement) at the University of Melbourne and was formerly head of the Lowy Institute and dean of ANU's College of Asia and the Pacific. His books include *There Goes the Neighbourhood: Australia and the rise of Asia* and *Mind of the Nation: Universities in Australian life*.

Georgina Woods is a poet and environmentalist.

QUARTERLY ESSAY BACK ISSUES

- ☐ **QE 1** *In Denial* by Robert Manne $27.99
- ☐ **QE 2** *Appeasing Jakarta* by John Birmingham $27.99
- ☐ **QE 3** *The Opportunist* by Guy Rundle $27.99
- ☐ **QE 4** *Rabbit Syndrome* by Don Watson $27.99
- ☐ **QE 5** *Girt By Sea* by Mungo MacCallum $27.99
- ☐ **QE 6** *Beyond Belief* by John Button $27.99
- ☐ **QE 7** *Paradise Betrayed* by John Martinkus $27.99
- **QE 8** *Groundswell* by Amanda Lohrey OUT OF STOCK
- ☐ **QE 9** *Beautiful Lies* by Tim Flannery $27.99
- ☐ **QE 10** *Bad Company* by Gideon Haigh $27.99
- ☐ **QE 11** *Whitefella Jump Up* by Germaine Greer $27.99
- ☐ **QE 12** *Made in England* by David Malouf $27.99
- ☐ **QE 13** *Sending Them Home* by Robert Manne with David Corlett $27.99
- ☐ **QE 14** *Mission Impossible* by Paul McGeough $27.99
- ☐ **QE 15** *Latham's World* by Margaret Simons $27.99
- ☐ **QE 16** *Breach of Trust* by Raimond Gaita $27.99
- ☐ **QE 17** *'Kangaroo Court'* by John Hirst $27.99
- ☐ **QE 18** *The Worried Well* by Gail Bell $27.99
- ☐ **QE 19** *Relaxed & Comfortable* by Judith Brett $27.99
- ☐ **QE 20** *A Time for War* by John Birmingham $27.99
- ☐ **QE 21** *What's Left? by Clive Hamilton* $27.99
- ☐ **QE 22** *Voting for Jesus* by Amanda Lohrey $27.99
- ☐ **QE 23** *The History Question* by Inga Clendinnen $27.99
- ☐ **QE 24** *No Fixed Address* by Robyn Davidson $27.99
- ☐ **QE 25** *Bipolar Nation* by Peter Hartcher $27.99
- ☐ **QE 26** *His Master's Voice* by David Marr $27.99
- ☐ **QE 27** *Reaction Time* by Ian Lowe $27.99
- ☐ **QE 28** *Exit Right* by Judith Brett $27.99
- ☐ **QE 29** *Love & Money* by Anne Manne $27.99
- ☐ **QE 30** *Last Drinks* by Paul Toohey $27.99
- ☐ **QE 31** *Now or Never* by Tim Flannery $27.99
- ☐ **QE 32** *American Revolution* by Kate Jennings $27.99
- ☐ **QE 33** *Quarry Vision* by Guy Pearse $27.99
- ☐ **QE 34** *Stop at Nothing* by Annabel Crabb $27.99
- ☐ **QE 35** *Radical Hope* by Noel Pearson $27.99
- ☐ **QE 36** *Australian Story* by Mungo MacCallum $27.99
- ☐ **QE 37** *What's Right?* by Waleed Aly $27.99
- ☐ **QE 38** *Power Trip* by David Marr $27.99
- ☐ **QE 39** *Power Shift* by Hugh White $27.99
- ☐ **QE 40** *Trivial Pursuit* by George Megalogenis $27.99
- ☐ **QE 41** *The Happy Life* by David Malouf $27.99
- ☐ **QE 42** *Fair Share* by Judith Brett $27.99
- ☐ **QE 43** *Bad News* by Robert Manne $27.99
- ☐ **QE 44** *Man-Made World* by Andrew Charlton $27.99
- ☐ **QE 45** *Us and Them* by Anna Krien $27.99
- ☐ **QE 46** *Great Expectations* by Laura Tingle $27.99
- ☐ **QE 47** *Political Animal* by David Marr $27.99
- ☐ **QE 48** *After the Future* by Tim Flannery $27.99
- ☐ **QE 49** *Not Dead Yet* by Mark Latham $27.99
- ☐ **QE 50** *Unfinished Business* by Anna Goldsworthy $27.99
- ☐ **QE 51** *The Prince* by David Marr $27.99
- ☐ **QE 52** *Found in Translation* by Linda Jaivin $27.99
- ☐ **QE 53** *That Sinking Feeling* by Paul Toohey $27.99
- ☐ **QE 54** *Dragon's Tail* by Andrew Charlton $27.99
- ☐ **QE 55** *A Rightful Place* by Noel Pearson $27.99
- ☐ **QE 56** *Clivosaurus* by Guy Rundle $27.99
- ☐ **QE 57** *Dear Life* by Karen Hitchcock $27.99
- ☐ **QE 58** *Blood Year* by David Kilcullen $27.99
- ☐ **QE 59** *Faction Man* by David Marr $27.99
- ☐ **QE 60** *Political Amnesia* by Laura Tingle $27.99
- ☐ **QE 61** *Balancing Act* by George Megalogenis $27.99
- ☐ **QE 62** *Firing Line* by James Brown $27.99
- ☐ **QE 63** *Enemy Within* by Don Watson $27.99
- ☐ **QE 64** *The Australian Dream* by Stan Grant $27.99
- ☐ **QE 65** *The White Queen* by David Marr $27.99
- ☐ **QE 66** *The Long Goodbye* by Anna Krien $27.99
- ☐ **QE 67** *Moral Panic 101* by Benjamin Law $27.99
- ☐ **QE 68** *Without America* by Hugh White $27.99

QUARTERLY ESSAY BACK ISSUES

- ☐ **QE 69** *Moment of Truth* by Mark McKenna $27.99
- ☐ **QE 70** *Dead Right* by Richard Denniss $27.99
- ☐ **QE 71** *Follow the Leader* by Laura Tingle $27.99
- ☐ **QE 72** *Net Loss* by Sebastian Smee $27.99
- ☐ **QE 73** *Australia Fair* by Rebecca Huntley $27.99
- ☐ **QE 74** *The Prosperity Gospel* by Erik Jensen $27.99
- ☐ **QE 75** *Men at Work* by Annabel Crabb $27.99
- ☐ **QE 76** *Red Flag* by Peter Hartcher $27.99
- ☐ **QE 77** *Cry Me a River* by Margaret Simons $27.99
- ☐ **QE 78** *The Coal Curse* by Judith Brett $27.99
- ☐ **QE 79** *The End of Certainty* by Katharine Murphy $27.99
- ☐ **QE 80** *The High Road* by Laura Tingle $27.99
- ☐ **QE 81** *Getting to Zero* by Alan Finkel $27.99
- ☐ **QE 82** *Exit Strategy* by George Megalogenis $27.99
- ☐ **QE 83** *Top Blokes* by Lech Blaine $27.99
- ☐ **QE 84** *The Reckoning* by Jess Hill $27.99
- ☐ **QE 85** *Not Waving, Drowning* by Sarah Krasnostein $27.99
- ☐ **QE 86** *Sleepwalk to War* by Hugh White $27.99
- ☐ **QE 87** *Uncivil Wars* by Waleed Aly & Scott Stephens $27.99
- ☐ **QE 88** *Lone Wolf* by Katharine Murphy $27.99
- ☐ **QE 89** *The Wires That Bind* by Saul Griffith $27.99
- ☐ **QE 90** *Voice of Reason* by Megan Davis $27.99
- ☐ **QE 91** *Lifeboat* by Micheline Lee $27.99
- ☐ **QE 92** *The Great Divide* by Alan Kohler $27.99
- ☐ **QE 93** *Bad Cop* by Lech Blaine $27.99
- ☐ **QE 94** *Highway to Hell* by Joëlle Gergis $27.99
- ☐ **QE 95** *High Noon* by Don Watson $27.99
- ☐ **QE 96** *Minority Report* by George Megalogenis $27.99
- ☐ **QE 97** *Losing It* by Jess Hill $27.99
- ☐ **QE 98** *Hard New World* by Hugh White $29.99
- ☐ **QE 99** *Woodside vs the Planet* by Marian Wilkinson $29.99
- ☐ **QE 100** *The Good Fight* by Sean Kelly $29.99

Order back issues online

Prices include GST.
$10 flat-rate shipping within Australia.
Please include this form with delivery and payment details overleaf.
Back issues also available as ebooks from ebook retailers.